LEGACY IMPACT AUSTRALIA

THE PERSONAL LEGACY GUIDEBOOK

Published by:
Legacy Impact Australia
ABN: 69188945109
www.legacyimpact.com.au
legacyimpactaustralia@outlook.com

Title: The Personal Legacy Guidebook
ISBN: 978-1-7646428-0-4 (paperback)
ISBN: 978-1-7646428-1-1 (ebook)

A catalogue record for this book is available from the National Library of Australia.

Edit and design by Legacy Impact Australia.

This book is dedicated to those who wish to record their personal

legacy –

may these pages remind you that what you leave behind

continues to connect with the lives of others

Contents

WHY I WROTE THIS BOOK

I began this book after a series of events that changed the way I thought about memory, family and how a life is remembered.

It started with losing two grandparents within a few years of each other. The first grandparent I lost passed away in 2021, she was in her eighties and her passing was not unexpected. After she died, my dad sent me an extract from a short biography she had attempted to write that the family had found among her things. As I tried to read it, the cursive writing became harder to decipher and as the writing continued there were parts that were impossible to interpret. These were pieces of her story I could see existed but I couldn't access them, nor could many others. At her funeral, her sister gave a beautiful eulogy about how my grandmother had designed her wedding dress. It struck me that there were whole parts of her younger life that I wish I'd known and now would only ever be told of second-hand.

Not long after that, I lost my second grandparent. Again, her passing wasn't unexpected. At her funeral, no one from the family spoke, instead the speeches were provided to the funeral director. Our family had lived in different parts of the country for many years, and once the service ended, everyone returned home. If I wanted to know more about her life, it would need to be told through the few family photos I had or if I directly asked my mother. This is when I began to realise how quickly stories can narrow and how easily detail disappears.

Then in 2023, I almost lost my dad. For my whole childhood I had watched him dedicate himself to his corporate career. At the time, this was the traditional path many fathers followed, but it meant he missed many milestones along the way. As I grew older, I realised how little I truly knew about the man behind the role and how much of his story I only understood at a surface level. He is now in his mid-sixties and I am increasingly aware that there will come a time when I will have to prepare myself for life without him. I started to wonder whether my own children would ever really know him and who he was? But, how could they really know that if I didn't know it myself?

Becoming a mother also changes your perspective. I began thinking not only about preserving the stories of those before me, but about leaving something behind for my own children. If something happened to me, what would they know? Would they understand how the events of the last twenty years shaped my thinking? I would want to impart some wisdom on them, to know that they could still hear me even when I'm no longer around anymore.

That was when I started writing. I began documenting the experiences that shaped me, the moments I felt influenced by history, by work, by loss, by resilience, so that they could one day understand that people are shaped by the times they live in just as much as by their own personal choices.

That process is what led me to establish *Legacy Impact Australia*. Its purpose is simple: to help individuals capture, preserve and communicate their life stories and personal impact through professionally crafted legacy books. At its core, is a simple belief: that every life leaves a mark, and every person deserves the chance to preserve the story of why theirs mattered.

Our time on earth touches more people than we realise. Long after we are gone, our influence remains in the memories of others. A legacy book ensures that a life's impact is not forgotten. I wrote this so more people have the chance to preserve the stories that shaped them.

INTRODUCTION

It is widely cited in industry and survey data that more than 80% of people say they would like to write a book, yet fewer than 1 to 2% of people actually do. The truth is that writing is difficult, not because we lack stories, but because we often doubt whether we are the right person to tell them, and more importantly, how we should tell them.

Many people assume that writing a book requires perfect grammar, polished language or natural creative talent. It does not. A legacy book is not about producing a bestseller, but about recording the parts of your life that matter before time quietly edits them for you.

This book is designed to guide you through the process of writing your own legacy book without the pressure of being a "perfect writer." What we want to capture are the memories, lessons, values and moments that shape who we are so that they can be understood by those who come after us.

Many people delay writing because they do not know where to begin. They feel overwhelmed and unsure of how to structure it, or concerned they will 'do it wrong'. This book seeks to remove that uncertainty and replace it with a clear and practical framework.

It is separated into four parts:

Part One focuses on preparing to write your legacy book: the reasons why you have chosen to write, who you are writing for and what you want to write about.

Part Two explores the general process of writing your legacy book: including understanding the practical and logistical considerations involved in producing written work.

Part Three discusses options for how to structure your legacy book: helping you organise your experiences in a way that feels coherent and meaningful to make writing it easier.

Part Four is to write your legacy book: turning your reflections into written chapters and building momentum so your book is completed and not just imagined.

Remember that you do not need to be a writer to leave a legacy. You simply need to begin.

PART 1 – PREPARING TO WRITE

WHY DO YOU WANT TO WRITE A BOOK?

A legacy book is about preserving a life and making a conscious decision that your story will not be left to memory alone.

In preparation for writing a legacy book, it is essential to pause and reflect on three foundational questions:

Why are you writing it?
Who are you writing it for?
What do you want to write about?

These questions are structural in that they guide your content and determine the depth that you are willing to bring to the page for the people it is meant for.

When you are clear about these questions, your writing gains direction, your chapters begin to organise themselves naturally and your story forms. Without this clarity, a legacy book can easily become a collection of scattered memories.

To be remembered

For many people, the desire to write a legacy book is simple: they want to be remembered. Not in a grand or historical sense, but in a meaningful way that exists within families. They want to be remembered in a way that is not reduced to surface-level facts such as career milestones or professional titles. They want to leave something behind that reflects the person that they were and the roles that they played in someone's life.

A legacy book does this by explaining what shaped your thinking, what you learned through experience, what you might have done differently, and how you changed over the course of your life. Through the writing process, the deeper layers of a life begin to surface. Motivations, values, doubts, and flaws are brought to light. The reasoning behind life's choices becomes clear and what may have appeared straightforward from the outside is revealed as a layered life shaped by context, emotion and the realities of the time.

When you write with the intention of being remembered, you are preserving how you will be understood. A legacy book enables future readers, whether they are children, grandchildren, colleagues, or people who you may never have met, to understand your story and the time in which your life decisions were formed. They are no longer left to interpret your life through the accounts of others and instead are invited into your own reflections.

To write in order to be remembered is ultimately a gift that offers those who live on after you something richer than a summary of events, it offers an understanding of who you were rather than just what you did. It is not surprising that this remains one of the most common motivations for writing a legacy book because most of us hope that our story will continue to live on in the memories of those who come after us.

Case Example

Peter, a retired engineer in his seventies, began writing his legacy book after concerns that his grandchildren only knew him as an absent grandfather. He lived on the other side of Australia and was lucky to be able to see them once a year. Through writing, he documented his early years growing up in regional Australia, his career achievements, and the risks he took starting his own business. When his family later read his writing, they commented that they finally understood the determination behind the person they had always known but never truly saw. His story did not change how he was remembered, but it deepened how he was understood.

To preserve family history

Another powerful reason people choose to write a legacy book is the desire to preserve family history before it quietly slips away. Family history may be anything from stories about where particular members migrated from, the risks that were taken, the hardships or sacrifices made, and the defining moments that shaped future generations. Alternatively, it may be family stories of humour, holidays and everyday moments that you want to ensure are not lost in time.

Preserving family history offers younger generations a perspective on the resilience shown and the events experienced by those who came before them. I experienced this personally during the COVID-19 pandemic. When the uncertainty of 2020 unfolded, I found myself wondering whether my parents had ever lived through anything comparable. I was curious and seeking reassurance that this uncertainty had been faced before. In my case, my parents had not experienced anything similar. For the next generation, I am not sure if my children will face something comparable in their lifetime. They will most likely learn about the pandemic in a history class and wonder how it felt to live through it. I want my children to understand not only the facts of that time, but the emotional reality of it.

Writing a legacy book with the goal of preserving family history not only captures its story but also preserves what life actually felt like during a particular time. It records the way people spoke to each other, what they valued, the traditions they kept and what they hoped for themselves and their children. These details seem irrelevant when you are living inside of them but can become precious the moment they are gone. I often think about that now living through a cost-of-living crisis in a country where the birth rate is at a historic low. I wonder if what I am experiencing now is comparable to my great grandmother who looked after 14 children in the 1920s during periods of recession. I will never fully know, because nobody wrote it down.

One of the strengths of this type of writing is that it can go in any direction. You may choose to explore a deeper ancestry history or keep it to general experiences that occurred within the writer's lifetime. Overall, preserving a family history gives future generations a foundation to better understand how life evolved to where it is today.

To pass on lessons or inspire others

Over the course of a lifetime, lessons are learned, sometimes through success, often through failure, and almost always through experience. We may choose the wrong path many times and spend years trying to find our way back only to rediscover the original lesson. By the time we understand what those experiences were actually teaching us, we are usually years past them. A legacy book is a place to articulate those lessons clearly and thoughtfully.

If this is your reason, you might explain what you came to understand about the fundamentals of life, whether in work, relationships, health or financial responsibility and offer insight into how you navigated these paths. Alternatively, you may acknowledge where you made mistakes. Some of the most enduring lessons often come from misjudgements and you can reflect on what it felt like at the time compared to what you learned from it looking back.

Writing in this way is less about giving direct advice and more about sharing a perspective about what you have lived through. Readers may not share your exact circumstances, but they may recognise what shaped your decisions and see similarities between those same influences in their own lives. There is also a sense of comfort in knowing that your experience may spare someone else unnecessary hardship should the lesson be something similar. For example, you may provide a lesson about your experience in selecting an occupation that you enjoy rather than solely for money. That lesson tends to hold true over time and may be the advice someone needs to hear.

By passing on lessons and values through a legacy book, you are creating something future readers can turn to for guidance. A written reflection can be returned at any time, with each reading meaning something slightly different depending on where the reader is in their own life. Long after spoken advice has faded, a legacy book remains for present and future generations.

To leave something personal

For some, writing a legacy book is about leaving behind something personal that represents who they truly were. After someone is gone, what often remains are official records, photographs or second-hand stories told by others. While these have value, they rarely capture how a person actually thought, what they believed or how they experienced their life from their own perspective. A written account tailored to a particular person can be a personal gift that explains *'this is who I was, this is what mattered to me, and this is how I understood the world'*.

Leaving something personal shifts the focus from yourself to the person who will one day hold it. The person receiving it may be someone you know deeply or someone you may have never met who has no memory of your voice. Receiving a legacy book can provide a lasting connection that may be cherished across generations. The words you leave behind can touch, guide and influence another's life long after you are gone.

If this is your reason, you may wish to focus on writing in your natural voice rather than trying to sound formal or literary. The writing should reflect your natural voice so the legacy feels genuine and recognisably yours. Often the sections that readers value most are not the most polished and the small imperfections in how you express yourself can become part of what makes the book feel personal. Leaving something personal in a legacy book is what the people who love you are truly hoping for when they open it.

Case Example

Louise began writing her legacy book with the intention of leaving something her children could return to long after she was gone. Rather than focusing on major milestones, she chose to write

---

about the small things she hoped they would remember: how she always tried to make birthdays feel special, why she valued education, and the reasons she encouraged independence even when it was difficult to watch. She also included letters to each of her children describing what she admired most about them as individuals. Years later, she realised that what she left behind was something personal, so that they would always know how deeply they were loved.

To make meaning of your own life

For many people, writing a legacy book can become an unexpected way of making sense of their own story. Life is sometimes lived at a fast pace. Decisions are often made in the moment, without the luxury of stepping back to reflect on what they might mean later. It is only when one pauses and looks back that patterns begin to emerge.

When you start writing your life down, it eventually forms a holistic view in which you can see how one decision led to another, how certain experiences shaped your beliefs or how particular setbacks strengthened you in ways you did not recognise at the time. Events that once felt isolated begin to make sense in the context of who you are today, even though you could not see it at the time. Making meaning of your life can mean acknowledging the resilience you overlooked, the growth you took for granted, and how far you have come.

There is also something healing about reflecting back with honesty. Unanswered questions can be examined with maturity and age and you may discover that what once seemed like failure became a redirection, or that a difficult event shaped strengths that would later define you. I personally experienced this recently

when I had my second baby who was premature and born at 26
weeks. At the time I felt guilty and over analysed everything I
could have done differently. Over time I came to realise that while
the experience was extremely difficult it made me appreciate the
gift of being a mother even more. After going through the
experience, my outlook on worrying about the small things
changed, and I became a different person because of it.

Making meaning through writing is not about rewriting history but
interpreting it through hindsight. In this sense, a legacy book
becomes a way in which you can interrogate the various chapters
of your life to understand it more deeply and in turn make peace
with it.

To correct the record

Every family has turning points that shape the lives of those within
it as well as those around them, such as marriage, divorce or a
disagreement that changed relationships. For some, the desire to
write a legacy book emerges from a quiet recognition that parts of
their story have been misunderstood, oversimplified, or left
incomplete.

To correct the record is to provide context and explain what may
have been happening behind the scenes. This may involve
recording the pressures that were present, the information
available at the time, and what considerations shaped that
particular decision. Without that context, the people around you
are left to interpret your decisions through their own observations
and they will, because that is what people do.

The intention of correcting the record is not to have the last word.
It is about ensuring that your account of events exists by offering
your own voice to the record. You are ensuring that future readers

encounter a version of events that comes directly from you rather than through the accounts of others.

Every life contains moments that look different from the outside compared to how they may have felt from within. A career change may be viewed as ambition when it was driven by necessity; a family disagreement may be remembered as stubbornness when it was rooted in misunderstanding; and silence may have been interpreted as cruelty when it was pain. Writing allows you to articulate these events with calm reflection rather than the reaction that would have occurred at the time. While a legacy book cannot control how you are remembered, it does ensure that your voice remains part of the story.

<table>
<tr><td>

Case Example

Michael decided to write part of his legacy book after realising that some of his career decisions had been misunderstood by his family. When he left a stable role, some relatives believed he had acted impulsively. Years later, he explained that the decision had followed internal politics and being passed over for a position he was more than capable of performing. By documenting the circumstances, the risks he considered, and the responsibilities he was balancing at the time, he was able to provide context rather than justification. His intention was not to revisit what he felt the organisation had done 'wrong' by him, but to ensure that his decisions were understood within the reality in which they were made, whether people agreed with them or not.

</td></tr>
</table>

To strengthen the connection with immediate family members

Families are bound by shared stories, the ones told across dinner tables, during long car journeys, at weddings, or in moments of quiet reflection. They create a sense of belonging for those who share them. They remind individuals that they are part of a family unit and not on their own. These stories do not disappear all at once. They gradually fade unless someone chooses to preserve them.

Writing a legacy book can become a deliberate act of strengthening that connection. When you set down your experiences, you are showing that you are a person who had their own aspirations and struggles. Knowing that the person behind the story once wrestled with comparable doubts, softens the tendency to judge them solely by outcomes. Instead of seeing a family member as a fixed character, such as "the stay-at-home mum", "the strict father" or the "successful sibling", readers begin to understand the circumstances and values that shaped them into that perceived role.

When writing a legacy book to strengthen family connection, you are giving them something they may not have wanted to ask for directly. By explaining the moments that influenced you, the values you tried to live by and even documenting the experiences that you cherished together, those closest to you can see you as a whole person rather than simply the role you occupied in their lives. This deeper understanding can strengthen connection, even many years into the future.

In this context, a legacy book may not be for the grandchild who is reading it in thirty years, but the daughter reading it now, finally understanding why her mother made the choices she did. Sometimes the greatest value of writing your story is not just that it is read in the future, but that it brings understanding to the relationships that matter most today.

Because time feels limited

For many people, the decision to write a legacy book is not prompted by ambition, but by the awareness that comes when time no longer feels limitless. A milestone birthday, retirement, the birth of a grandchild, the loss of a parent, or a personal health challenge can sharpen this perspective. As I mentioned at the beginning of this book, in 2023 I almost lost my dad. His health scare frightened me. It made me realise that the conversations I thought would eventually happen won't unless he or I deliberately attempt to record them.

Time has a way of slipping past unnoticed. Years fill with responsibilities, careers, caregiving, and the ordinary demands of daily life which results in stories being postponed for a time when things feel quieter. Yet for many, as it did for me, that time never quite arrives. The recognition that time is not infinite can act as a clarifying force, bringing into focus what truly matters and why documenting it should not be delayed.

Writing in this context is not an act of fear, but a response to the understanding that memory is fragile and the opportunity to document it will not be available forever. When someone chooses to document their life because time feels limited, they are acknowledging the value of their experiences and the importance of preserving them while they still can. They are choosing to act while their voice and recollections are clear and their reflections have matured.

There is also something grounding about confronting the limits of time. It removes the desire to impress and replaces it with wanting to be authentic. When time is recognised as precious, the focus shifts from perfection to presence, and rather than crafting the perfect story we tend to leave something more real and meaningful behind. Ultimately, writing ensures that the stories that shaped you do not have to end when you do.

The good news is that you do not have to choose just one reason as to why you want to write a legacy book. Most people write from a combination of motives. Identifying those reasons is simply the first step. From there, you can decide who you are writing for and what you want them to understand. When those answers become clear, the structure of your book begins to take shape naturally.

WHO DO YOU WANT TO WRITE YOUR BOOK FOR?

Every book begins with a reader. Before you start writing, pause and ask yourself a simple but important question: *Who am I really writing this for?* The answer to that question will shape everything. It will influence your tone, whether you explain more or assume that they already hold a certain understanding, and how honest you allow yourself to be.

When we think of writing a legacy book, we often assume it means writing about ourselves. In truth, it is writing to someone. Perhaps a son or daughter who may one day wonder what you were like at their age. A grandchild curious about where certain traits came from. Or a partner who shared part of the same journey.

If you imagine a faceless audience, your writing becomes cautious and distant. If you imagine a specific person, you will naturally begin to organise them towards what you want to write about.

A question worth sitting with is:

> *Who do you want to hold your book one day and what do you want them to feel when they do?*

Writing for your children

When you consider who you are writing this book for, many people instinctively think of their children. Writing for your children requires a different kind of honesty. It asks you to imagine them not as they are now, but as adults perhaps reading your words twenty or even fifty years from today, at a stage of life where they may be asking questions they never thought to ask before.

If your children were to read your book decades from now, what would you most want them to understand about you? Beyond the daily routines of parenting, beyond the rules you enforced, what would you want them to see clearly? You may want them to understand the pressures you were under at the time, the responsibilities you carried, the sacrifices you never spoke about, or the hopes you held for their future. There are likely chapters of your life that would make far more sense if they were explained. These may be things such as career decisions, financial constraints, relocations or moments of stress. In those circumstances, your loved ones may only remember the outcomes. Writing is where you can explain the reasoning behind some of these decisions.

I have experienced the questioning that comes with parent choices personally. When I was ten years old, my parents moved cities. I was in year 6 at primary school, I had friends, and a life that felt permanent in the way only childhood can. I had no real understanding of how much change a single decision could bring and for years I resented the decision they had made to move the family. At the time, all I could see was what I had lost, not what was gained. Now, as an adult with children of my own, I see it differently. Perhaps they were seeking stability or a better future for our family. Those reasons may have existed, but they were difficult to explain to a ten-year-old who simply wanted things to stay the same. That is the power of writing with context.

Writing for your children can put into words the values you lived by, especially if you did not always speak them. Children may remember your work ethic, your kindness, or your independence and may question whether you also saw those qualities in yourself and why they mattered to you. There may also be things that you hope your children never have to guess such as expressing your love for them or whether you were proud of them. Life does not always create space for these conversations, but writing does.

Writing for grandchildren or people not born yet

There is something profoundly humbling about writing for someone you may never meet. When you write for grandchildren or for generations not yet born, you are placing your voice into the future and trusting that one day, someone will open these pages and get to know who you were.

Writing for the future invites you to consider how you wish to be understood within the context of your era and what it felt like to live through it. They will not understand the pressures of your time unless you describe them. I did not fully appreciate this until I thought about my own family. As I wrote in the opening of this book, there is more that I would have liked to have known about my nanna. She was one of 14 children. As an adult living through a cost-of-living crisis, and when the birth rate historically low, I often wonder why the experience of being a mother was different at that time, particularly in the 1940s. To have heard her perspective would have provided insight into the life lived within that time.

When I think of my nanna, I think of someone I knew only partially. A name, a face, a handful of memories. Imagine a relative of your own finding your photograph decades from now and knowing nothing more than that. Would you want them to understand more about who you really were? This is what a legacy book can offer. It gives you a chance to tell your story and to say *'This is what shaped me. This is what I learned. And this is what I hope you carry forward. Or perhaps do differently'.* A legacy written in this way can transform a memory into a connection so that even as families grow and change, the people who came before them are never completely lost.

Writing for a partner or close loved one

Writing for a partner or a close loved one carries a different weight from writing for future generations, because it is less about explaining who you were in history and more about articulating who you have been within a shared life. When you write for the person who has stood beside you, whether for years or for decades, you are not just recording events, you are deepening understanding and giving voice to parts of yourself that the pace of everyday life leaves little room to express.

In long relationships, sometimes emotions may not have been spoken because life does not create many natural openings for that kind of honesty. Writing gives you somewhere to put the things you have been meaning to say for years. These may be things such as admiration for navigating difficult times together, gratitude for continuing to choose the life you built together and acknowledgement of what it cost the other person to stay. In doing so, you ensure that what existed between you is not left to assumption but recorded in your own words, in your own voice.

Writing for a loved one may also be a way to honour enduring friendships and to reflect on the memories you have gathered together over time, because some relationships stretch quietly across decades and become woven into family life. There are friendships that have lasted since the birth of children, where families have been raised alongside one another, navigated milestones and setbacks together, and accumulated a shared history.

Overall, writing for someone you have loved is an appreciation of what is particular to this person, this relationship, this shared history that nobody else would know to record. That specificity is what makes it worth writing and worth keeping.

Writing for parents or elders

Writing for your parents or for those who came before you can carry a particular tenderness, because it sits at the intersection of history and identity. Unlike writing for children or grandchildren, where you are explaining yourself forward in time, writing for parents often involves looking backward. It involves tracing where you came from, how you were shaped, and where your path gently or decisively diverged from theirs. It can be one of the most courageous forms of writing, because it requires both truth and compassion.

As adults, we make choices that our parents did not always understand. There may be decisions you made about career, relationships, where you chose to live, whether to have children and which values we kept from your upbringing and which ones we set aside. These choices may have been the result of motivations that your parents gave you to explore those opportunities not given to them or the fact that you simply choose to pursue a different path. Writing offers an opportunity to explain *'this is what informed my decision and this is where I needed to step into my own life'*.

Within this space, there is often room for gratitude, reconciliation, and recognition. Gratitude for sacrifices that may only be visible now that you stand in adulthood yourself; recognition of strengths you inherited but once took for granted; and reconciliation for misunderstandings that lingered, not out of malice, but out of a failure to understand one another. The writing is not about changing the past, it is about placing it within your perspective. In doing so, your legacy book can hold what life may not have allowed you to articulate: appreciation, apology and love.

Writing for yourself

Although many people begin a legacy book believing they are writing for children, partners, or future generations, it is not uncommon to discover along the way that the most important audience is far closer than expected. Beneath the desire to preserve stories for others, often sits a quieter need to understand your own life more clearly.

Some experiences that we move through rather than process because that is what the situation required. When we survive difficulty, we rarely pause to ask ourselves whether it altered something within us. We simply continue. It is often only years later, sometime decades, that we notice how resilient we were, or how profoundly a single period shaped the person we became. Writing offers the opportunity to return to those moments not to relive them, but to finally make sense of them.

There is also something freeing about writing with no audience in mind. When you write for others, even with the best intentions, you are always making choices about what to include, what to soften, and what to leave out. When you write for yourself, those filters can come down. That shift alone can surface memories and feelings that have been waiting a long time for somewhere to go.

As you reflect, you may begin to recognise that certain moments shaped your behaviour and influenced your choices more profoundly than you realised at the time. These may include a failed marriage, cycles of abusive relationships, financial difficulties or just mental insecurities. These are not always the stories we lead with, but they are often the ones that explain the most about who we are and how we move through the world.

Writing gives those feelings somewhere to land. It allows you to sit with them, to trace where they came from and where they led, and to look at yourself with the kind of patience you may not have extended to yourself at the time. Many people find that the act of articulating something difficult, even privately, brings a sense of coherence that years of simply carrying it did not.

There are also stories people may hold privately for a long time. Doubts about choices made, ambitions that were set aside, or fears that were never shared widely because it felt unsafe to show vulnerability . These do not need to be written for anyone else to read. In fact, some of the most honest writing in your process may never make it into the final book, and that is entirely appropriate. The value is in the writing itself, in the acknowledgement that these experiences existed, that they mattered, and that they contributed to who you became. Even if no one else reads those words, the act of articulating them can bring coherence and self-reflection.

Once you know who you are writing for, the story begins to organise itself to what you want to be written. The person you are writing for will then influence your tone, the level of detail, and the emotional weight you give certain memories. In moving from audience to content, you step into the heart of the writing process, this is where the book begins to take shape not as a collection of events, but as a life story.

WHAT DO YOU WANT TO WRITE ABOUT?

Once the why and who questions have been answered, you generally have direction as to what you want to write about and this in turn can assist in determining your story.

Recording a life story

Most people, when they first consider writing their legacy book, say they want to record their life story. It is easy to understand why. There is something reassuring about that instinct — the idea that if we capture everything from childhood to the present, nothing important will be lost.

Writing a life story often covers decades, but it may move quickly across certain periods in order to maintain balance. For example, a chronological life story can be easier to structure if organised by the life stages of childhood, young adulthood, parenthood and then to later life. You may begin with a reflection on the environment you grew up in, any expectations that were placed on you and the opportunities that were either given or denied. These are the things that would have shaped your beliefs, decisions and character. A reader who understands those conditions will understand your decisions differently than one who only knows the outcomes.

It is natural when writing a life story to want to fit everything into a single volume. The practical risk of this format is that the sheer scope of a life that can work against you. When there is a lot of ground to cover, it is tempting to keep moving to record what happened with a description rather than sit with why it mattered and provide more reflection. The best full life stories resist that temptation by pausing at significant moments to explore them in greater depth. Depending on your approach you may create separate volumes for each life stage, however taken together they tell the story of how your experiences shaped the person you became.

Overall, the format doesn't matter much as long as you capture the experiences that shaped you, the lessons you carried, and the moments that mattered most. What you choose to record becomes a bridge between your experience and the understanding of those who will one day read it. In doing so, you are not only preserving what happened, but explaining what it was like to be you – at that time, in those circumstances, making decisions with what you knew then. That is something no one else could have written.

Recording a focused story or a particular life event

Not every legacy book needs to span an entire lifetime. Some of the most powerful stories are built on a specific chapter of their life such as a serious illness; a marriage breakdown; a business failure; a period of political or corporate leadership or raising children with particular challenges.

A focused story trades breadth for depth, but the depth it requires can also make it the hardest kind of writing. Instead of moving across decades at a steady pace, it stays inside one experience long enough to actually examine it — what led to it, what it felt like from the inside, and what it eventually taught. That kind of stillness takes courage. It means resisting the urge to summarise and instead allow the experience to unfold.

The structure of a focused story tends to follow the natural arc of the experience itself. If the subject is illness, your story might begin before the diagnosis — in the small signs that were easy to dismiss — and move through treatment, uncertainty, and whatever came after, whether that was recovery, adaptation, or loss. If the subject is a marriage breakdown, it might trace the quiet distance that grew before anything was spoken aloud, through to the eventual separation and the process of rebuilding a sense of self on the other side. The beginning and end points are yours to define, but the most honest focused stories tend to start earlier than the obvious moment and end later than the resolution, because that is closer to how life actually unfolds.

I want to write one of these myself. I have two premature children and there is a story in those early weeks that I have never fully told — not because I do not know it, but because I have not yet been ready to sit inside it again. Those weeks held a particular kind of fear, the sort that does not announce itself loudly but settles into the body quietly and stays there until I enter into a hospital or medical environment again. I know the shape of the story I want to tell -I know where it begins and roughly where it ends. What I have not yet found is the steadiness to write it without the weight of it pulling the words in directions I am not emotionally ready to return to.

Some chapters require distance before they can be written. It is an honest acknowledgment that emotional readiness and timing matters as much as anything else when the subject is something that still carries weight. Writing from too close can sometimes produce work that is raw in ways that serve the writer but not yet the reader. If the chapter you want to focus on is one you are still processing, it may be worth starting somewhere else and returning to it when the distance feels sufficient. You might begin with an easier period, or a different subject entirely, and find that the writing itself gradually prepares you for the harder material. The story will wait. It is not going anywhere.

Recording your professional life

A professional life occupies a significant portion of our lives and for some people can become connected to their identity. It is therefore unsurprising that many people feel compelled to document their professional journey as part of their legacy.

Recording your professional life is not about producing an extended version of your resume. It is a reflection of your professional contribution that may explore the responsibilities you carried, the principles that guided you, the ethical tensions you navigated, and the lessons you learned in positions of leadership. It gives you the opportunity to explain not only what you did, but why you did it, and potentially what sacrifices it required at the time. These experiences often intertwine with wisdom, and a legacy book allows you to record the insight you accumulated over your career.

What makes this format work is that professional life tends to organise itself naturally. Careers move through defined chapters — roles, projects, leadership phases — which gives the writing a structure that a full life story sometimes lacks. This can be particularly valuable for those who have worked in governance, public service, corporate leadership or community organisations, where decisions influence others long after the role concludes.

There is also something worth saying about relevance. Insight accumulated over decades has a habit of disappearing quietly when someone steps away from formal responsibilities. In this way, a legacy book can be provided as an ongoing resource for colleagues, successors or emerging leaders within the same field that offers guidance grounded in experience rather than procedure.

It is also worth noting that a professional legacy may narrow the audience. Colleagues and industry peers may find your book highly useful but family members or future generations will likely connect more deeply with the personal reflections than with organisational detail.

Legal and ethical sensitivities may also arise as professional life often involves confidential information and care must be taken to respect privacy, avoid defamation and honour obligations that may still apply which can limit how openly certain events are described.

A legacy book that reads like an annual report has missed the point. The most enduring professional legacies tend to be the ones that show both - what the work was and who was doing it, and what it cost the person who came home at the end of the day.

Case Example

Sandra spent over thirty years working in local government and decided to document the professional lessons she had learned. She wrote about difficult decisions, ethical tensions, and the importance of being professional when under pressure. She also provided insight into the blurred line between senior leadership and political pressures which she thought could help future leaders. While her family appreciated understanding this part of her life, she found that former colleagues returned to it more as

---

it offered practical experience which they found useful while navigating their careers.

Recording of your life lessons and wisdom

For some, the strongest motivation for writing a legacy book is to preserve what an experience has taught them. Recording your life lessons and wisdom is the act of gathering those accumulated insights over decades and placing them into words.

A lessons-based legacy does not move through time in sequence, instead it is re-arranged around themes such as leadership, relationships, money, integrity, faith, or purpose. It is underpinned by the values you lived by, the moral boundaries you refused to cross, and the traditions you hope will continue long after you are gone. The result is an account of life experience - less concerned with what the achievements were and more concerned with what they taught.

This structure enables the writer to draw from multiple areas of life without feeling bound to recount every detail. It can make the writing process more focused and manageable, particularly for those who wish to highlight what mattered most rather than reconstruct a full life story. Another strength is timelessness. Lessons often remain relevant and resonate across generations, even as circumstances change. Recording lessons and wisdom also enables the writer to speak directly to the reader and provide insight into life experiences that may shorten another person's learning curve. For family members, it can feel like a private inheritance of guidance.

This structure does have its limits. When lessons are offered without the stories behind them, they can feel detached rather than guided. Wisdom lands differently when the reader understands where it came from. For this reason, an integrated approach is often the better choice to capture both professional life and the lessons from it.

Recording an integrated legacy of professional and personal life experiences

Most lives do not divide neatly into either a professional or personal category. An integrated legacy recognises that the two intersect - family responsibilities may have influenced career paths just as career demands may have shaped family dynamics. My own background sits at exactly this intersection.

In relation to my integrated legacy, I spent years working in government, building my resume and attempting to climb the corporate ladder. That work shaped how I think and the skills I have today but the higher I tried to climb the more disconnected from the work I became because it no longer complemented my personal qualities. That is why I structured Legacy Impact Australia around two streams. The first being the personal legacies that tell the story of who a person is; and the second being the professional legacies that reflect the achievements that change the world and the personal qualities of what it took to do that. That is what an integrated legacy looks like, a cohesive portrait of experience.

When writing an integrated legacy, you may examine: how your early upbringing may have shaped your leadership style, how family responsibilities may have affected career decisions, how your personal ethics may have informed professional judgement, and how professional setbacks may have changed your personal priorities. Structurally, this format can move chronologically through life stages, showing how professional and personal life developed in parallel. Alternatively, it may be organised around themes such as responsibility, resilience, service or sacrifice.

This format is often particularly meaningful for individuals whose work carried significant responsibility or public visibility, yet whose private life sustained or shaped that work. When both are present and genuinely integrated the reader gains a full account of what it actually cost and required to live that particular life. For these legacies, family members may connect with the personal reflections, while colleagues and peers engage with the professional insight. The result is a story that speaks to both readers.

Privacy is the primary limitation of this approach. When discussing the intersection of work and family which involve other individuals, those stories intertwine within your own. As a result, sensitivity, discretion and consent all matter when sharing your own experience while remaining thoughtful about its impact on the people who share parts of it.

Case Example

Erin was a qualified lawyer and senior governance manager for several years. One day she was told that her contract would not be renewed. She had always performed well and was never given any indication that she was unable to do her job. As it was a senior contract, she was unable to argue unfair termination and as hard as the decision was, it was one she had to accept. She knew the reason she was let go was her inability to play politics. She decided to write a legacy book for her children that integrated both her personal and professional life. In her legacy she acknowledged that she had lived by the ideals of the law. Integrity was the one value she refused to compromise, even when it came at a professional cost.

Recording general traits

Not every legacy book must revolve around events, milestones or formal achievements. Some people may want to leave behind a sense of who they were- their disposition, their temperament, the habits that defined them.

General traits are the things people remember about you long after the details fade. They include qualities like humour, spirituality, the things that stressed you, what you were drawn to, and how you honestly assessed your own strengths and weaknesses. These qualities are often the most vivid memories a family carries because they do not attach themselves to specific events – they are simply the things that make you who you are. By capturing these traits, you can offer future generations a clearer understanding of your identity.

One of the genuine advantages of this approach is that it doesn't require the writer to reconstruct a full chronology. Patterns and reflections are often easier to identify than precise events, which can make the writing feel more manageable. The risk, however, is writing traits in the abstract. Describing yourself as resilient without ever showing what that resilience looked like in practice leaves the reader with a label rather than a person. The traits need at least one story behind them.

A legacy book built around character gives future readers a sense of the person behind the events. It preserves not only what you experienced, but how you chose to respond. That tends to be the part of a legacy book that gets read more than once.

Recording for the future and not the past

There is a difference between writing about your past and writing for someone who will encounter it as history. When your grandchildren read about your life, they will not understand the world you were navigating unless you describe it. This may involve describing what society felt like in your era, the economic realities, political climates or technological limitations and how this context shaped your decisions.

Recording for the future requires context-setting. It involves explaining the assumptions that guided your thinking at the time and the environment in which you operated. If you changed careers, describe the economic conditions that influenced that decision, or if you made a controversial choice explain the cultural climate that framed it. By doing so, you preserve not only your story, but the atmosphere in which it occurred.

I think about this when I consider what I would have wanted to know about my grandmother. She was one of fourteen children, born in the 1920s. I want to understand what it meant to be a mother in that era — not just the facts of it but what was expected, what was feared, what was simply accepted as the shape of a woman's life at that time. That context would change how I understand her. It would change how I understand myself. She never wrote it down, and so I am left to wonder.

Writing for the future means accepting that the reader will need more explanation than you think. What may feel obvious to you because you lived through it will be invisible to someone reading decades later. Ultimately, this perspective strengthens a legacy book so that your story is not only remembered - it offers insight into the world as you knew it and the reasoning behind the life choices you made.

Recording expressions of love

Many people begin writing a legacy book for practical reasons but beneath the desire for order and explanation lies an emotional desire to express love. Love may not always have been spoken directly during the busiest times of our life; responsibilities, ambition, hardship or restraint may have limited what was expressed aloud. A legacy book creates the opportunity to express affection, gratitude and admiration in ways that daily life may not have always allowed.

Love in a legacy book can take many forms. It may be directed toward a spouse or partner whose steady presence shaped the direction of your life; or may be addressed to children offering reassurance, encouragement and pride; or may honour parents whose sacrifices created opportunity; or may acknowledge loyalty to a community that commanded long-term devotion. These are an honest record of what one person felt about another and tend to be the parts readers return to the most.

Recording love also humanises the broader life story. Achievements and lessons gain texture when placed within the broader context, for example, a professional milestone may carry different meaning when framed alongside appreciation for family support. Some writers may choose to include direct letters within their book, pausing within it to speak directly to specific individuals. These sections are often among the most treasured because they replace observation with direct address and the tone becomes personal and unguarded.

What makes this approach powerful is also what requires care. Words of love directed to some and not others can create unintended hurt, so thoughtfulness about who is included matters as much as what is said. But when handled well, it gives future readers not only an understanding of your life, but how you felt about the people within it.

Recording a tangible history

Reflection forms the heart of a legacy book, but there is unique power in preserving tangible evidence alongside it. Family photographs, newspaper clippings, personal letters, official documents, diary excerpts or certificates - each item serves as a fixed point in time, grounding memory into documented reality.

Tangible elements do more than decorate a book. A photograph captures the expression and the setting of the time; a letter preserves tone from a specific moment; a newspaper clipping provides the broader public context; a diary entry reveals thoughts that were felt at the time. These artefacts transform recollection into documented history.

These materials can be integrated throughout the story or presented in dedicated sections. Some writers choose to embed photographs or letters within relevant chapters, while others include appendices or visual galleries. Timelines can provide clarity, especially when multiple life events intersect with broader historical developments. When thoughtfully arranged, these materials enrich rather than interrupt the flow of the story.

One unique advantage is preservation. Physical artefacts are vulnerable to loss, damage or dispersal over time and including them within a legacy book safeguards them. These tangible items also carry emotional weight - seeing the faces of ancestors or reading words written decades earlier creates an immediate sense of connection to the reader that tends to draw them deeper into the story.

The practical side requires effort. Gathering, scanning and organising materials takes time, and privacy and legal considerations may arise when including personal letters or images that involve other individuals. These are manageable challenges, but worth anticipating rather than discovering halfway through production. None of the effort is wasted. A tangible history preserves more than memory alone, it secures pieces of the past in a form that can be held, returned to and passed on.

PART 2 – GENERAL PROCESS FOR WRITING A BOOK

WHAT WRITING A LEGACY BOOK ACTUALLY INVOLVES

Before exploring structure, editing, or publication, it is helpful to understand what the process of writing a book actually involves. For many people, the idea of "writing a book" feels intimidating and may provide assumptions of having to be disciplined and producing polished chapters, however the process is far more flexible and accessible than most people imagine.

Writing a book sounds enormous until you break it down. At its core, writing a book is not a single act but is a sequence of stages that build on each other gradually until it becomes a tangible product. It begins with determining why you want to write, who you want to write for and what you want to write about. The process then shifts to gathering thoughts and memories which are gradually shaped into a loose chapter structure. Drafting follows, which may involve writing chapters out of order, or only putting a few dot points on the page to begin.

The process then moves into reviewing what you have written. In this stage you may be clarifying details, expanding or rewriting content and ensuring that the overall story on the page matches the one you intend to tell. After the story has been refined, the editing phase begins where the draft is carefully reviewed for structure, punctuation and overall readability, ensuring that the final version reads professionally. The final stage is presentation which decides how the book will be formatted, shared, or preserved. It is important to recognise that these stages are not strictly sequential as you may move back and forth between them.

A book rarely comes together in a single attempt. It evolves over time by choosing to return to it. By understanding the stages involved, you can approach your book with the patience to work through each stage gradually.

The following are some general processes worth considering before you begin your legacy book.

Time and commitment (without pressure)

When people begin to consider writing a legacy book, one of the first concerns they have is whether they will actually have the time to complete it. Many assume that writing a book demands large, uninterrupted blocks of time and a disciplined daily routine, and then abandon the idea when they realise that the expectation becomes incompatible with the realities of real life. As a result, they often stop before a single word is written.

It is important to reframe the expectation of writing a book. A legacy book is not a deadline-driven project but one that develops gradually over time. Writing may consist of an hour once a week, or half a page each month. These contributions feel insignificant in the moment but they do accumulate. Missing a week does not break that commitment. There will be periods of momentum and periods of pause, and both are natural in the writing process.

Writing must fit into the life you already have. You may be working full-time, raising children, caring for others, or making time for other personal interests. A legacy project should not compete with these responsibilities, nor should it require you to withdraw from them. In many ways, it is written alongside life rather than separate from it. It is entirely reasonable for the process to extend over a year, two years, or longer.

Give yourself permission to write slowly. By maintaining a consistent commitment to returning to the page, you create conditions in which progress can unfold organically. In this way, your legacy book becomes less a task to be completed and more something that you will want to return to.

Emotional readiness

Writing has a way of reopening things. Many people underestimate this. They assume that because an event occurred years ago that it has been fully processed, however writing has a way of resurfacing feelings as details return. This is not a sign that something is wrong but a natural consequence of the reflection process.

In the context of writing, emotional readiness does not mean that every chapter of your life must be perfectly resolved before you begin, rather, it means having the self-awareness to approach those moments that may have been more difficult with self-kindness. You may feel entirely comfortable writing about your early career yet hesitate when approaching memories of personal disappointments. It can be helpful to begin with stories that feel grounded and stable before gradually moving toward more complex material as your confidence grows.

Emotional readiness also involves considering the audience you are writing for. If your book will be read by children or grandchildren, you may need to reflect carefully on how certain experiences are framed. For example, if you are writing about a marriage breakdown between you and your spouse, and they are your child's parent, you may choose to approach the subject with some discretion rather than recounting the entirety of the relationship in a negative tone. In doing so, you maintain the relationships that continue beyond the page.

In many ways, writing a legacy book becomes an exercise in emotional maturity. It calls on you to reflect not only on what occurred but on how you understand it now. Time may have softened judgements, or clarified motivations or reshaped what certain experiences meant. The version of events you can offer now is often more useful because it is reflective. When you approach your writing with this mindset, you allow the wisdom gained from that experience to become part of what you leave behind.

Case Example

When David began writing his legacy book, he had every intention of including an honest account of his first marriage and the circumstances that ended it. What he had not anticipated was how difficult he found writing it. After several attempts that left him unsettled for days afterward, he decided to write around it, documenting everything else first and returning to it when he felt ready. When he was able to write that chapter he wrote it exactly as he experienced it but because it was deeply personal to him, he never included it in the final book. Instead, he wrote a single private letter to himself that he kept separately. He found that the act of writing it, even for himself, gave him the ability to not just see his ex-wife's mistakes but his own as well.

Self-kindness

In the process of writing a legacy book, one of the most important qualities you can develop is self-kindness. While structure and reflection all have their place, the tone you adopt toward yourself will shape both the experience of writing your book and the voice that emerges on the page. Many people approach personal writing with an internal critic, one that questions the value of their story, the quality of their language, or the accuracy of their perspective.

Self-kindness begins with approaching your writing with gentleness rather than judgment. That shift alone creates an environment in which your voice can surface more freely. There will inevitably be moments when the words feel clumsy, when a memory seems incomplete, or when you struggle to articulate something that feels clear in your mind. This is a natural part of the writing process. This may also involve adjusting expectations as some chapters may be shorter than anticipated or others may be larger than they need to be. Self-kindness gives you permission to write imperfectly, knowing that first drafts are not final and that refinement will come later.

It is equally important to extend compassion toward the earlier versions of yourself who appear in your story. When revisiting decisions made years ago, it can be tempting to judge them through the lens of present understanding. Hindsight offers clarity, but it can also bring harshness. Writing with self-kindness means remembering that every decision was made with the information, capacity, and perspective available at that time.

Self-kindness also acknowledges that the writing will not always feel easy. There will be weeks when progress is slow, when a chapter resists being written, or when you simply cannot find the words for something you know you want to say. A legacy book written with compassion toward yourself tends to read differently from one written under self-imposed pressure. When written with self-kindness, the voice is warmer, the honesty comes more naturally, and the reader can feel the difference.

Finding your voice

One of the most common concerns expressed by those beginning a legacy book is uncertainty about how they should sound. Many people assume that writing a book requires adopting a more formal tone and this assumption can create hesitation as you may begin to measure your words against an imagined standard of what "an author" sounds like, rather than trusting your own expression. The purpose of a legacy book is to preserve your voice rather than reshaping it into an artificial version. Your life has been lived in your voice and it deserves to be recorded in that same voice.

The people who will one day read your words, whether children, grandchildren, colleagues, or future generations want to recognise the tone they associate with your guidance, your stories, your explanations, and the way you see the world. A voice that feels natural will always be more enduring than one that feels formal and constructed unless that tone fits your personality and is actually how you would have written it. One practical way to approach this is to write as though you are speaking to the specific person or persons you have chosen to write your book for.

It is also helpful to accept that your voice may evolve across the pages of your book. When recounting early childhood memories, your tone may feel descriptive and observant but when writing about professional decisions, it may become analytical and measured, and when reflecting on family relationships it may carry warmth. This variation is not inconsistency; it reflects the many dimensions of a life.

Case Example

Comparing the opening of two versions of the same story

Stiff and formal:

The house in which I was raised could be described as rustic in character. Certain areas had fallen into a state of disrepair over time. The property contained a wood-burning fireplace which, when lit, would raise the ambient temperature of the room considerably. During the winter months I would sit nearby and consume tea and biscuits.

In a natural personal voice:

We didn't have much growing up, but it never felt that way to me. The house was small and a little run down, but it was cosy. We had an old woodfire and I used to love sitting next to it on winter nights.

Selective disclosure

When something is placed in writing, it shifts from a passing memory into a lasting record. Deciding to write a legacy book does not mean that everything must be told, particularly when considering the privacy of others.

There may be aspects of your life that involve other people's private experiences and those stories are not yours alone to fully document. In legacy writing, being selective acknowledges that there may be ongoing relationships with others and that what we write can have lasting consequences. It can be helpful to ask yourself several questions before including any sensitive material, such as:

- Does this detail serve a meaningful purpose in understanding my life?
- Will this detail affect existing relationships?
- Would I feel comfortable if this were read by anyone involved?

These questions are not designed to stop you, but to ensure that what remains on the page is relevant to the overall story.

In many cases, you may acknowledge that a relationship was difficult without reproducing conversations or reopening arguments or you may note that a professional disagreement shaped your path without assigning blame. Your legacy book is not lessened by what it does not contain. In many ways, what you choose not to include can be just as thoughtful as what you decide to record.

Case Example

Disclosed without care:
My brother and I had a falling out in 1987 over money that was left to us by our parents. He took more than his share to pay off his drug debt. I think he used all the money he had on buying drugs from the tobacco store on High Street. His actions damaged our relationship permanently and I think he knew what he was doing.

Disclosed with care:
My brother and I went through a difficult period in the years after our parents died. Grief does complicated things to families, and ours was no exception. In the final settlement he was provided a

Accepting incompleteness

Writing a legacy book does not need to be perfect to be valuable. If you waited until every chapter felt fully resolved, every memory was fully examined, and every relationship was perfectly explained, you would likely never finish. Accepting incompleteness is not the same as accepting carelessness. It is an acknowledgement that you are capturing a life to the best of your ability, and that this is enough.

Memory is selective by nature. Dates blur, details fade, and conversations are recalled through the filter of how they felt at the time rather than how they unfolded word for word. When you are writing a legacy book, you are offering the details to the best of your recollection, not the exact reconstruction of events that occurred. A legacy book is complete when it communicates your perspective, your reasoning, your values, and your experiences and nothing more. The finished product might not be perfect but is complete because it has been written by you.

PRACTICAL THINGS TO CONSIDER

Before you begin recording personal memories, family stories or professional experiences, it is important to pause and consider the legal circumstances around publication. Writing a legacy book may feel personal, but once words are printed or shared, they become part of a public and permanent record with legal implications. This does not mean you should write with fear but instead be aware of any consequences your words may bring. Understanding the basic legal considerations allows you to protect yourself, respect others, and ensure your story can be shared responsibly.

Understanding defamation

When writing about real people, particularly those who are still living, it is important to understand the concept of defamation. In simple terms, defamation occurs when you publish material that harms another person's reputation by presenting false statements as fact.

In Australia, defamation law applies not only to newspapers and broadcasters, but also to books, memoirs and even privately distributed publications. If a reader could reasonably identify someone from your description, even without a name, and the material damages their reputation, there is potential legal risk.

Understanding that there is some caution in writing does not mean you cannot tell difficult or honest stories. Legacy writing may involve disclosing conflict, mistakes, and people whose behaviour caused harm to you. However, you should take care to:

- Distinguish clearly between fact and opinion.
  To do this, you may use language that reflects your experience as you recall it. For example: 'To the best of my recollection' or 'In my view this is what happened as I experienced it';

- Avoid exaggeration or emotionally charged claims presented as objective truth.
  Instead, you may want to frame difficulties as the feelings you had during that experience. For example: 'There were difficulties during that period that placed a strain on me' or 'I remember feeling'.

- Consider whether allegations can be substantiated;
  Instead, you may describe the behaviour. For example: 'I experienced behaviour that was frightening' or 'There were times where I felt unsafe' or 'His actions made me feel like'.

For a legacy book the defamation risk would be relatively low. The audience is small, the distribution is limited, and the purpose of your book is preservation rather than accusation. Circumstances where the risk increases are more likely for those stories that relate to your professional life where the occupational reputation of someone would be greatly impacted if there were negative written accusations.

In those cases, some ways of telling your story while writing about particular people may include changing identifying details, describing how you felt at the time, using more general descriptions of relationships, or choosing language that reflects your perspective without making accusations. For example: you may say things like, 'in my experience' or 'I felt' or 'At the time it seemed to me that' or 'At the time I believed that'.

Another way of showing caution may be to include a gentle disclaimer at the beginning of your book. For example, 'Certain names and identifying details have been changed to respect privacy' or 'This book reflects my personal recollections and perspective, written in good faith'. This has become somewhat of a common practice when writing memoir books to avoid seeking consent, particularly where such persons may only be a small part of the whole story.

If you are looking to pivot your book commercially or your book will be widely shared you may consider seeking consent from those mentioned in the book or obtaining legal advice. Defamation law is not designed to silence your story but it is designed to protect reputational harm. With thoughtful drafting, careful language, and a commitment to fairness, you can tell your story while remaining legally aware.

Copyright

Copyright is the legal protection that applies to original creative works including writing, photographs, letters, artwork, newspaper articles, and even diary entries.

In Australia, copyright automatically belongs to the creator of the work at the time it is created (unless it was produced in the course of employment or assigned by agreement). This means that even if you physically own an old letter, a photograph, or a newspaper clipping, you may not own the copyright of it. That is, ownership of the object is different from ownership of the intellectual property.

When writing a legacy book, copyright issues most commonly arise in three areas: reproducing photographs, quoting from letters or diaries, and including extracts from published works such as newspapers, books or speeches.

Before including full documents, lengthy quotations, or images created by others, you should consider whether you need permission from the copyright holder. You cannot reproduce substantial parts of someone else's work without permission unless an exception applies, such as fair dealing, which relates to research purposes. In Australia, copyright generally lasts for 70 years after the author's death.

For most legacy books, the 70-year rule is unlikely to be relevant, but it is worth being aware of when including older published material. The following are practical ways to manage copyright responsibly:

- Use your own original writing and photographs wherever possible;

- If using another person's material, use short quotations only;

- Use material that is in the public domain;

- Summarise or describe documents rather than reproducing them in full.

If you intend to publish commercially or distribute your book widely you may consider seeking consent.

Overall, respecting copyright is not about restricting your story, it is about acknowledging creative ownership. A legacy book can still include rich historical context and meaningful artefacts, but doing so thoughtfully ensures your work is both ethically and legally sound.

When to change names and details

There are circumstances where changing a name and identifying details is not only appropriate, but wise. In legacy writing, you may be recounting events that involve sensitive family dynamics, workplace conflict, personal hardship, or behaviour that could harm someone's reputation or privacy if made public. Even where your account is honest, altering names and certain identifying details can reduce legal risk and prevent unnecessary distress.

Changing a name alone is not always enough. A person can still be identifiable through their role, location, relationship to you, timeframe, or the specific facts of an incident. To anonymise someone, you may need to adjust multiple elements such as occupation, physical description or the story setting. Overall, you might consider changing names and details when:

- The person is still living and has not consented to being included;

- The story involves allegations, misconduct, or deeply personal matters;

- The events could expose someone to embarrassment or reputational harm;

- Children or vulnerable individuals are involved; or

- You are recounting workplace or professional disputes.

If you have changed names or minor identifying details to protect privacy, consider noting this in a brief disclaimer at the beginning of your book.

For a family legacy book shared only within a close circle, the practical risk of including real names is relatively low but if there is any possibility the book will be shared more widely, changing names and adjusting identifying details is a simple precaution that requires very little time. It is a simple precaution that protects both your voice and the dignity of others.

Gentle disclaimer language

Most family legacy books will not require a disclaimer. But if your story contains material that could identify someone in a negative light, even without naming them directly, a brief note at the front of the book is a simple and sensible precaution. In some circumstances, the absence of a disclaimer may increase the risk of a defamation claim.

A gentle disclaimer helps clarify that names may have been changed and reasonable efforts have been made to respect privacy. It manages expectations for the reader without undermining the integrity of your work.

Other examples of disclaimers that may be used include:

- 'This book is based on my own personal memory, recollections and perspective';
- 'No harm or misrepresentation is intended by the statements within this book';
- 'This book reflects my personal recollections and perspective. Where memory and documentation differ, I have written in good faith and to the best of my knowledge';
- 'Within this book every effort has been made to acknowledge the creators of photographs and materials.

Where the photographer or copyright holder is unknown, I welcome contact for proper attribution'.

These examples can be used individually or combined depending on what your book contains. The language within your legacy book does not need to be formal. What matters is that it is genuine in its intention to respect the people within it.

Photos

Photographs can transform a legacy book. A single image can anchor memory in a way that written words sometimes cannot. For future generations, photographs are often the first pages they turn to as they give history a face.

Copyright in this context is relevant. If you took the photograph yourself, you generally own the copyright. If someone else took the photo, even a family member or a professional photographer, the copyright may belong to them.

If the person who took the photograph has died, copyright does not disappear, as it generally lasts for 70 years after the death of the creator. That means the rights to reproduce the image usually pass to their estate, which may be a spouse, children or the beneficiaries under a will.

If you do not know who took the photograph, the image is considered an "orphan work" meaning the copyright owner cannot be identified or located. This does not automatically mean the photo is free to use as the copyright still exists even if the rights holder is unknown.

For a family legacy book, the risk of copyright and privacy is relatively low. However, you may choose to reduce the risk by doing the following:

- Use the image with a note such as: *"Photographer unknown. If you hold copyright in this image, please contact the author"*;

- Describe the photograph in text rather than reproducing it, such as who is pictured, when it was taken, and why it matters; or

- Replace it with an image you own the rights to.

The legal side of photographs is worth understanding, but it should not discourage you from including them. Most family legacy books sit well within the boundaries of private use, and the practical steps above are usually sufficient. A photograph handled carefully is still a photograph worth including — and for many readers, it will be the part of your book they return to most.

The use of Artificial Intelligence (AI)

Artificial intelligence is increasingly being used as a writing aid to structure ideas, refine language, or overcome writer's block. In the context of a legacy book, AI can be a practical tool. It can help turn notes into paragraphs, suggest prompts, and provide editorial feedback. For many people who do not consider themselves "writers," it can assist them with beginning to write.

However, AI is the tool, not the author. It does not possess your experience or emotional voice, but generates language based on the prompts you give it. For that reason, any content produced with the assistance of AI should be reviewed carefully for accuracy, tone and authenticity. The responsibility for the final words remains with you, your legacy is to be told in your voice, not an automated system.

There are also important considerations around privacy and confidentiality. If you are using an online AI platform, be mindful of the information you input, particularly if it involves sensitive personal details as this information may be used to train the system how to manage such conversations. Ensure that you understand the platform's data policies and are comfortable with how your material is handled. Also avoid uploading documents that are legally protected or subject to confidentiality obligations without proper clearance.

From a legacy perspective, the central question is authenticity. If AI assists you in articulating your thoughts more clearly, it can be valuable. If it begins to replace your voice, it can undermine the purpose of your legacy. Overall, if you choose to use AI, consider it an editorial assistant to clarify, structure and refine but ensure the meaning, judgement and experiences remain unmistakably your own.

PART 3 – HOW DO YOU WANT TO COLLATE AND STRUCTURE YOUR LEGACY BOOK

OPTIONS FOR COLLATING YOUR BOOK

Before a legacy book can be written, the material must first be gathered and structured. This stage is less about producing polished chapters or refining language and more about collecting the moments and experiences that shaped a life and bringing them into one place.

Collating your legacy book is a practical and reflective process. It requires you to open boxes that may not have been touched in years, to scroll through archives of photographs and messages, and to begin mapping the events, relationships, and turning points that have formed your life.

For some, memories will come easily and for others they may need prompting. Similarly, some documents will confirm what you remember and others may demonstrate how flawed memory can be. At this stage, it does not matter if the material feels incomplete or out of order. Simply begin.

Memory mapping

Before you attempt to organise your story into chapters or themes, it is worth stepping back to look at your life as a whole rather than as a sequence of isolated events. Memory mapping is a practical way to do this.

To start a memory map, write your name or the title of your legacy book and place it in the centre of a large sheet of paper. From there, draw lines outward like branches to form separate categories. These will represent the broader domains of your life such as family, career, education, health, faith, community involvement, or any other categories that feel significant to you. These are not meant to be chapter headings but are simply starting points for recalling memories.

From each branch, develop smaller branches (sub-branches) to capture specific memories, relationships, events, or lessons that are connected to that area. For example, under the career branch, you might list the jobs you have held but then in the sub-branch you may note a pivotal job offer, a resignation, a career change, or a mentor who changed your thinking. Under the branch of family, you might record immediate family members, births and deaths but in the sub-branch you may list any relocations, reconciliations, traditions, or tense relationships.

The purpose of memory mapping is visibility. You may discover that certain branches expand rapidly while others remain limited, or you may notice that themes repeat across different areas of your life. These repetitions are worth paying attention to as these will likely become the central themes in your writing. In this way, memory mapping begins to reveal not just what happened in your life, but how your experiences connect and what patterns have emerged over time.

You may wish to repeat this process more than once, by creating one map focused on chronology and the other on themes or lessons. There is no single correct method, and this exercise can also reduce the intimidation of beginning your legacy book. When faced with a blank document, it is easy to feel that you must know where to start and how you will finish, but a memory map removes that pressure, as you are not locked into a starting point and can move freely between decades, recording multiple memories without committing to an order.

What matters is that you give yourself the opportunity to observe your life from a distance to see its scope and the way different parts of your life connect, and to recognise that even ordinary experiences form a pattern when viewed as a whole. What appears scattered at first often reveals a shape once it is all in front of you. Seeing your life mapped out visually often makes the act of writing feel more approachable than staring at a blank page.

Memory boxes and tangible material

A memory box can refer to two ways to collate your story. The first is as straightforward as finding a box and writing down memories as they come to you. For example, you may get a rectangular box and as memories come to you write them down on small cue cards which are then placed into the box. As you remember memories, you begin to order them with each memory either taking place before or after the last. Over time these memories will form the structure and substance of your legacy book.

The second method is collating physical items into a box. These might include a photo, a letter, a program from a graduation, a hospital bracelet, or a newspaper clipping. These items can powerfully inform and enrich your legacy book.

Creating a memory box in this respect is both practical and reflective. As you gather these objects, take the time to label them by writing the date, the location, the people involved, and any context that might be relevant. When the time comes to shape your story you will not be relying solely on memory, as you will have something physical to return to.

While the memory box will primarily serve as material for your legacy book, you may find it becomes something worth preserving alongside it. Some writers choose to present both together, allowing the reader to experience not just the story but the objects that mattered to you.

Photo albums

Photographs hold a unique power within a legacy book because they capture not only faces and places, but a particular moment in time that was worth preserving. A thoughtfully assembled photo album can become more than decoration within your legacy book; it becomes a record of the life you are describing.

When approaching your photo collection, begin by gathering images from across the full span of your life rather than focusing only on milestone events. Weddings, graduations and awards are important, but so too are ordinary afternoons, family holidays, work environments and community gatherings. It is often these everyday images that future generations value most because they reveal how life was actually lived.

When organising your photographs, consider whether they should follow the same structure as your written chapters. If your book moves chronologically, photographs arranged in the same sequence create a reading experience where the words and images speak to each other — the reader encounters a chapter about your school years and turns the page to find the photograph your parents took on your first day. In practical terms, where possible scan originals at high resolution before they deteriorate further. A digitised copy not only protects the original but also allows you to integrate photographs seamlessly into a printed book.

A photograph does not replace what you have written; it complements it. Words provide the interpretation and context while photographs provide the visual experience of how life was viewed at that time. When photos are integrated into your legacy book, they become a visual connection for future readers to not only understand your story but to see it.

Journaling

While photographs and documents preserve the visible outline of a life, journaling preserves the inner thoughts and feelings. A journal captures not only what happened, but how it felt at the time.

If you have written in a journal revisit it as the contents are often far more revealing than memory alone because they were written close to the moment of experience. You may rediscover ambitions you had forgotten, fears that you no longer hold or views that remain unchanged while others have shifted. Some of these reflections may never appear in your final book, but they will deepen your understanding of your own growth. If you have not previously kept a journal, it is not too late to begin.

When collating your legacy story, an old journal shows you how you actually felt at the time rather than how you remember feeling in retrospect. When reviewing your journal, write down how you described your feelings during particular situations that occurred at the time.

With the benefit of hindsight, you can revisit your initial reactions, consider how your thinking may have changed over time, and reflect on how you now understand that experience. For instance, when discussing relationships, you might include a journal extract of your first heartbreak, or when writing about marriage, an entry capturing your nerves or joy of the night before the wedding day.

Overall, journaling slows down the writing process in a constructive way. It creates space between the experience and the account of it. Most people find that what they felt at twenty-five about a particular event and what they understand about it at sixty are genuinely different things. A journal gives you access to both versions. A legacy book gives you the space to hold both of those versions at once. Many writers find that revisiting old journals makes the writing feel less like reconstruction and more like a genuine conversation with an earlier version of themselves.

Look back over your social media

For many people, particularly in the past fifteen to twenty years, a significant portion of their life has been recorded online. Social media platforms have quietly become informal archives of milestones, opinions, celebrations, grief, travel, professional achievements and everyday observations. When collating your legacy story, it may be worth recognising that your digital footprint may contain material as telling as any letter or photograph you might have kept.

To collate material for your legacy book, begin by approaching your social media history as an archive and scroll through earlier years, paying attention to posts that marked transitions such as a new job announcement, a relocation, the birth of a child, or a moment that touched everyone. These posts often contain timestamps, photographs and reflections that can help you piece together not just when things happened but how they felt. You may rediscover how you described an event at the time, which can be just as emotive as a journal extract as it is your voice in real time.

There are also practical considerations. Platforms change, accounts close, and data can be lost. Should you want to refer to these posts in your legacy book it may be helpful to download archives of your content and store them securely. If you intend to reproduce posts, comments, or images within your legacy book, make sure that you consider the privacy implications, particularly where other individuals are tagged or quoted, such as in a family group chat. In these instances, you may want to paraphrase rather than reproducing them directly.

As a legacy book has no fixed format, social media posts and images can be integrated creatively to reflect both your story and the needs of your future reader. This may be particularly useful if writing for the younger generations who use social media as their primary means of communication.

Decide what belongs and what doesn't

One of the most confronting stages in collating a legacy story is not gathering material, but deciding what to include. When you begin this process, you may feel that everything matters because it is yours. Every achievement, every hardship, every disagreement, every private thought may appear equally deserving of space.

A legacy book can be any length but high-level memoirs tend to be around 300 pages. Therefore, you do not need to have an archive of everything that ever occurred unless that is the form you want to preserve, it can be shaped by selecting what best represents your life, your values, and the meaning you wish to pass forward. That selection is itself a choice only you can make.

A helpful question to ask is *"Does this contribute to the understanding of who I am?"* Some events are significant in the moment but do not reflect the direction your life took. Others may seem small at the time yet reveal something essential about your character, your motivations, or your growth. In this context, whether it belongs is not determined by the size of the memory but by relevance to who you want to convey and how you wish to be understood.

When collating your materials, you may encounter repetition as certain themes or stories may appear in multiple forms but are told in different ways. For example, you may have gathered some journal entries that detail your inner thoughts about a situation and then find some social media posts that describe the same situation on a surface level. This is where you may keep both items but when writing your story find which one best serves the story you are telling.

Deciding what belongs requires you to step briefly into the role of editor as well as that of storyteller. It asks you to consider audience, impact, tone, and your overall legacy. The goal is not whether something should be included but whether it aligns with the story you are choosing to tell. While there is no set format, careful selection ensures that what remains on the page feels purposeful and worth passing on.

STRUCTURING YOUR LEGACY BOOK

Structure is often the part that causes people to hesitate before a single word can be written. Structuring provides a gentle framework that organises your thoughts to bring order so that the content can be absorbed and understood.

When thinking about the structure in a legacy book, you are not deciding how to impress a publisher; you are deciding how best to guide someone you care about through your life in a way that feels clear. Creating structure shapes your story to serve its reader –
and there is more than one way to build that shape well.

There is no 'correct' structure

One of the most common beliefs about writing is that there must be a particular structure to follow before you can begin, and as a result, many people delay starting because they feel they have not yet identified the "correct" framework from which to write. However, in legacy writing, there is no single structure that governs how a life story must be presented, because no two lives unfold in identical ways and no two families read stories in quite the same manner.

Unlike academic essays or commercial publishing, a legacy book is judged less on technical precision but by its meaning to the author and the way in which it speaks to its reader. The purpose of a family legacy book is to communicate your life in a way that future readers can understand, rather than to satisfy a literary standard of perfection. Structure, in this context, is simply what keeps your story readable — a way of ensuring that memories land with meaning rather than accumulating as loose detail.

Life itself is rarely experienced in a tidy, chronological line. We remember in fragments, for example, a present-day event may pull forward a memory from childhood, or a conversation with a child may recall an experience you had at the same age. Just as our memories are layered rather than linear, it is entirely acceptable for your writing to reflect this same reality rather than laying out experiences into an artificial order simply because it feels more formal to tell it that way.

What matters most is that your legacy structure supports the understanding of its intended reader. If your reader can follow the journey, if they can see how one experience of life connects to another, if they can trace how certain decisions or values developed over time, then the structure is doing its job. There is no 'correct' structure, and your story may begin at birth, at a defining moment, or in the present reflecting backwards, so long as the framework you adopt supports the meaning you wish to convey.

For many writers, the structure of a book emerges through the act of writing itself. You may begin without a structure and find that as you write the patterns begin to reveal themselves which can then be adjusted, refined, and rearranged. Letting go of the idea that there is a right way to begin makes it easier to actually start.

Chronological structure

The chronological structure is the most familiar and instinctive way to tell a life story because it mirrors how we are often taught to understand history itself: beginning at the start and moving forward through time. In this approach, your story unfolds from childhood into adolescence, from early adulthood into work and relationships, and eventually into the reflections and understandings that come with later years. For many readers, particularly children and grandchildren, this format feels steady and reassuring because they can see how one stage of life leads into the next.

A chronological structure can clearly anchor memories to approximate dates, places, and life phases, which can be especially helpful when you are documenting family history. Readers are able to track your growth and over the course of reading understand how earlier experiences shaped later decisions. Writing in this structure also makes it easier to explain what the world was like at the time, how it changed, what opportunities or constraints existed, and why certain choices made sense.

A chronological structure can also reduce overwhelm for the writer. Instead of deciding what emotional theme to explore first, you simply begin at a natural starting point such as birth. In this context, you might open with your earliest memories, describe your parents and the environment in which you were raised, and then gradually move forward. The structure itself provides momentum, guiding you through your own timeline without requiring complex planning.

A chronological structure can also be used as the foundation of a book and what happens within it is yours to shape. For instance, it does not require strict adherence to a perfect sequence as you may occasionally step forward in time to offer reflection, then return to the moment you were describing. Alternatively, you may pause the story to explain how you now understand an event differently than you did at the time.

If you are uncertain where to begin, a chronological structure is often the most common starting point as it provides order without demanding complexity, allowing you to build your story layer by layer. You can always refine, rearrange, or expand later, but beginning with the simple question, "What came first?" is often enough to start writing.

Practical Example: Applying the Structure

Suggested chapter outline:

- Chapter 1: Family Origins
- Chapter 2: Early Childhood
- Chapter 3: School Years
- Chapter 4: Young Adulthood
- Chapter 5: Major Life Turning Points
- Chapter 6: Later reflections

Suggested opening sentence:

"My earliest memories begin in a modest house, full of laughter and family gatherings."

Suggested chapter structure:

- Begin by introducing the setting or period of life
- Follow with specific memories or experiences of that time.
- Include reflections or lessons that you now recognise from where you stand now.
- Conclude the chapter by transitioning to the next stage of life.

Decade structure

Similar to a chronological structure, the decade approach organises your story into ten-year periods. Chapters may be titled by the calendar year, for example: 'The 1980s' and so on or they may be the writer's age such as 'My 20s' then 'My 30s'. Within each decade, the writer reflects on the experiences, themes and events that defined that period of life. This approach still follows the chronological path broadly, but tends to be more flexible in its view of time rather than on the precise sequencing.

For many writers, this structure can feel natural because people often remember their lives in terms of periods rather than individual dates. A decade may be remembered as a time of establishing a career, raising young children, travelling, or facing particular challenges. By grouping memories within these ten-year blocks, you can explore the overall historical atmosphere of that time, what responsibilities dominated daily life and what priorities guided your decision-making.

A decade structure can also make the writing process more manageable. Instead of feeling pressure to recall every event in exact order, the writer can reflect on broader patterns that defined each period. This may include describing the places you lived, the people who were most present in your life at the time, and the significant events that occurred during those years. The chapter becomes less about documenting every moment and more about capturing the essence of that stage of life.

For readers, decade-based chapters can provide a clear structure for understanding how a life developed over time. Readers are able to see the progression of responsibilities, relationships, and personal growth across different periods. In this way, the story moves forward while still leaving space for reflection, helping the reader understand not only what happened but what it made of the person writing it.

Practical Example: Applying the Structure

Suggested chapter outline:

- Chapter 1: The first decade – childhood and early family life
- Chapter 2: The teenage years – identity and independence
- Chapter 3: My twenties – education, work and early adulthood
- Chapter 4: My thirties – establishing family and career
- Chapter 5: My forties – responsibility and changing priorities
- Chapter 6: My fifties – reflection and perspective
- Chapter 7: Later years – what life has revealed

Suggested opening sentence:

The 1950s: "My earliest memories are from around 3 years old. I remember the smell of my mother's cooking, the layout of my home and my bedroom full of toys. Most days followed a familiar and comforting pattern – wake up, breakfast, get ready for school, go to school, come home and have afternoon tea by the TV, dinner and then bed."

Suggested chapter structure:

- Begin by describing where you were at the start of the decade and what your life looked like at that time.
- Introduce several significant experiences or milestones that shaped those years.
- Include ordinary moments or routines to reveal what daily life truly felt like.
- Reflect on how your thinking and priorities changed during the decade.
- Conclude by acknowledging how that decade prepared you for the next stage of life.

Thematic (event) structure

A thematic structure moves away from the single timeline and instead organises your story around events that were significant to you. In this approach, chapters take shape from a specific moment such as an experience at high school, a first job, marriage, having a child, or an employment position that taught them their greatest lesson.

In this structure the chapter titles would reflect the events you want to explore with the depth a chronological structure rarely gives you. Such titles may cover things like: moving to the city for university; my first management role; my first heartbreak; meeting your mother or father; the day I became a mum; or taking a chance. In this structure, titles like these help readers quickly recognise that each chapter captures a moment that influenced the direction of the writer's life. Over time, these moments collectively form a story that reveals how different experiences shaped you.

For the writer, a thematic structure allows you to begin in a non-sequential order, starting where your energy feels strongest, which can reduce the pressure of the writing process. This structure can also help maintain momentum, as you are not bound to one section at a time. If your attention shifts or certain memories feel difficult to approach, you are free to move to another theme without interrupting the overall progress of the book. These sections may also be shorter than the chapters a chronological structure produces and over time these individual sections begin to form a fuller book.

For the reader, an event-based structure can make a legacy book particularly engaging because each chapter centres on a meaningful moment rather than a broad stretch of time. Readers often find this approach enjoyable because each chapter functions almost like a self-contained story. As they move from one event to another, they begin to gain a deeper understanding of the writer's character and values that influenced the direction of their life.

This structure works best for those who want to write about the lessons learned through particular events, or who want to weave together the major moments of both their personal and professional life.

Practical Example: Applying the Structure

Suggested chapter outline:

- Chapter 1: The move that changed everything
- Chapter 2: The job that shaped my path
- Chapter 3: Meeting the person who became my partner
- Chapter 4: Becoming a parent
- Chapter 5: A period of unexpected challenge
- Chapter 6: A moment that changed my perspective

Suggested opening sentence:
"The moment I received that email, I realised that the direction of my life was about to change. It was the day university offers were released."

Suggested chapter structure:

- Begin by explaining what was happening in your life leading up to the event.
- Describe the moment or situation itself, including the people and circumstances involved.
- Reflect on how you responded at the time and what you were thinking or feeling.
- Consider what the experience taught you or how it changed your path.
- Conclude by reflecting on how you understand the event now.

From the present-day structure

A present-day structure opens a legacy book on the day that you begin writing it. You might begin by describing your current life – your age, your surroundings, your family (as they are today) or the reason you have chosen to write at this particular moment. This grounding in the present gives readers context before they travel backwards with you through the earlier parts of your life.

This structure establishes your voice in active conversation with the reader rather than narrating your life from a distance. A simple opening such as "As I write this today, I am 58 years old..." can immediately bring the story to the present and provide context for what prompted you to write it, and what you hope your reader will one day understand from it.

The structural advantage of this approach is that the present becomes a point where you can choose to move forward or backward, explore themes, or explore events that led to the present situation. The present therefore becomes a reference point that you can occasionally return to at the end of each sub story to touch on how your understanding has evolved over time. This layered movement between now and then often deepens your story, because it highlights what you've learned rather than simply recounting events.

The practical risk of this approach is that frequent movement between past and present can cause the overall story to feel fragmented if the writer does not return clearly to the present before beginning the next section.

This structure can be therapeutic for writers as it acknowledges that you are not writing as the person you once were. Writing in this way can provide an opportunity for the writer to reflect on earlier chapters of life, recognising how certain events shaped their own character, values, and decisions.

Practical Example: Applying the Structure

Suggested chapter outline:

- Chapter 1: Where life stands today
- Chapter 2: The family and life I have built
- Chapter 3: The path that led me here
- Chapter 4: Early adulthood and major decisions
- Chapter 5: Formative years and influences
- Chapter 6: Childhood beginnings

Suggested opening sentence:

"As I write these words today, I find myself looking back over the many paths that gradually led me to the life I now live."

Suggested chapter structure:

- Begin by describing your current stage of life, including family, surroundings or daily routines.
- Explain what prompted you to begin writing your story at this point in time.
- Reflect briefly on the distance between the person you once were and the person you are today.
- Introduce the idea that the following chapters will explore the path that led to this moment.
- Conclude by gently transitioning into the earlier stages of your life.

A summary of lessons structure

Another way to structure a legacy book is to organise it around the lessons your life has taught you. In this approach, each chapter is built around a principle that has emerged through experience - something you have come to understand about work, relationships, integrity, resilience, ambition, or responsibility. The story then unfolds through the experiences that taught that lesson, rather than as just events.

Developing this structure begins with reflection. You might ask yourself: *What do I know now that I did not know at twenty? What has proven true across different stages of my life? What would I want someone I love to understand without having to learn it the hard way?* From those questions, a series of guiding statements can form the backbone of your book. Each chapter can open with a lesson which may be plainly stated then followed by the experiences that shaped it. For example, a chapter may be titled around the lesson of 'when one door closes, another one opens', from there the experience may be about job rejection and an unseen opportunity that led to a different path.

The practical strength of a lessons structure can be particularly powerful in a legacy context because it offers readers the insight you gained. This structure gives the writer room for reflection to acknowledge where things could have been managed differently in life, where there was innate confidence in decisions or where you are still learning. Even if the lessons are common, the events that led to them are personal.

Organising a legacy around a summary of lessons shifts the focus from what happened in life to what it meant. It recognises that the value of a life is not only in the story but in the wisdom it provides. For many readers, especially children and grandchildren, these are often the sections readers return to the most because they hold your advice on how to live.

Practical Example: Applying the Structure

Suggested chapter outline:

- Chapter 1: The importance of perseverance
- Chapter 2: The value of family
- Chapter 3: Learning from failure
- Chapter 4: The importance of kindness
- Chapter 5: Choosing integrity
- Chapter 6: What truly matters in the end

Suggested opening sentence:

"One of the most important lessons life has taught me is that perseverance often matters more than talent."

Suggested chapter structure:

- Begin by introducing the lesson or principle.
- Share experiences or moments from different stages of life that contributed to this understanding.
- Reflect on how your perspective evolved over time.
- Consider how the lesson influenced later decisions or relationships.
- Conclude by expressing what this lesson means to you now.

Letters within the structure

Letters can sit within a legacy book in a way that changes its emotional tone, because it shifts the narrative from description to direct connection. While the broader structure may move chronologically or thematically, a letter interrupts that flow to direct the reader to a single moment.

There are several ways letters can be woven into the structure without disrupting the overall story. Writers may choose to gather all letters into a final chapter, creating a deliberate closing section that speaks directly to children, partners, parents, or future generations. Others may choose to place letters immediately after the chapters they relate to. For example, a chapter describing a difficult career decision might be followed by a short letter to your children explaining what you hope that choice will one day mean for them or it may impart some advice on how to go about choosing a career.

Letters do not have to be long, they can be short and scattered throughout the book, appearing as brief interludes. A paragraph beginning with "If you are reading this..." or "What I hope you know..." can soften a chapter and draw the reader closer to what you are leaving behind. These moments break the formality of writing and remind the reader that this is not simply a record of a life but a relationship continuing across time.

One practical consideration is that a letter written to a specific person often contains shared history, or private understandings that belonged to the two of you. For readers who were not part of that history it can create a gentle distance rather than the connection the letter intended to create. It is worth considering, when writing to one person, whether the broader meaning of the letter can still be felt by someone reading from the outside.

Similarly, when multiple letters address different individuals in detail, this can slow the overall momentum of the book if the reflections become lengthy. Letters work best when they are placed at natural pauses within the book such moments you want to specifically reflect on, or those people you want to directly speak to.

Practical Example: Applying the Structure

Suggested chapter outline:

- Chapter 1: Childhood and early family life
- Letter: To my children about where our family began
- Chapter 2: Leaving home and early independence
- Letter: To my younger self about the choices ahead
- Chapter 3: Building a career and a family
- Letter: To my partner about the life we created
- Chapter 4: Later reflections
- Letter: To future generations

Suggested opening sentence:

"My dear children, I have often wondered what parts of my life story might one day help you understand where our family began."

Suggested chapter structure:

- Begin by addressing the person you are writing to and why you are writing to them.
- Share a memory, reflection or message that you hope they will understand.
- Offer insight, encouragement, or perspective drawn from your experiences.
- Acknowledge your relationship with the reader or the connection you hope they will feel.
- Conclude with a closing reflection or expression of love.

Generational structure

A generational structure shifts the focus of writing about one life, and places your story within your family's journey across generations. It might begin with grandparents or even great-grandparents, move through your parents' lives, arrive at your own experiences, and then extend forward to your children and grandchildren. The emphasis is not only on what you lived, but on what was inherited and what will be passed on.

This structure can be particularly meaningful in a legacy book because it answers questions that individual memoirs often leave untouched such as *Where did our family's values begin? What patterns repeat across generations? What sacrifices were made before I was born? What strengths or struggles seem to travel through our line?* By tracing these threads, your life becomes part of a larger story, shaped by those who came before you and shaping those who follow.

Writing in this way often changes the tone of the account. There is usually greater context because the story does not revolve solely around a personal achievement. Instead, it recognises that identity is formed within family systems, cultural environments, and shared histories. A chapter on your childhood, for example, may be framed by what your parents were navigating at the same age, which may in turn have been influenced by the upbringing they received. The generational structure naturally invites gratitude, understanding, and sometimes reconciliation.

Practically, this structure can be organised in generational segments or might be written around shared themes such as migration, education, or work, outlining how each generation responded differently to similar challenges. A generational structure is especially powerful for creating something for future generations who can return to it to understand where they came from and how their story began long before they arrived. In doing so, the book becomes not only a reflection of one life but a look into many.

Practical Example: Applying the Structure

Suggested chapter outline:

- Chapter 1: The generation before me – my grandparents' lives
- Chapter 2: My parents' generation and the world they grew up in
- Chapter 3: My own life and experiences
- Chapter 4: The generation of my children
- Chapter 5: Reflections for future generations

Suggested opening sentence:

"Long before I was born, the foundations of our family story were already being shaped by the lives of my grandparents. I have the records of my grandfather who travelled to Australia from Ireland in 1921."

Suggested chapter structure:

- Begin by describing who belongs to that generation and the period of history they lived through
- Introduce key experiences or circumstances that shaped their lives.
- Reflect on how their values, decisions or challenges influenced the next generation.
- Include memories, stories or family traditions that have been passed down.
- Conclude by explaining how this generation shaped your own life or the lives that followed.

Place based structure

A place-based structure organises your legacy book around the locations that shaped your life. Instead of asking "What happened next?" you ask, "where was I when I became who I am?" Chapters may be built around towns, houses, workplaces, countries, or even particular rooms that hold memory.

For many people, memory is inseparable from environment. A setting such as a childhood home, an office, a hospital corridor, or a coastal town, can carry emotional weight. This approach can be especially powerful when your life has involved movement such as migration, relocation, career transfers, or even shifts between rural and urban life. A chapter titled after a town or city can explore not only what occurred there, but who you were in that setting and whether you returned to it differently over time.

A place-based structure can also incorporate sensory writing that appeals to the five senses, helping the reader experience a scene rather than to simply understand it intellectually. This may include describing the visual environment, the sounds that filled the space, distinctive smells, the feel of physical surroundings and any memory of taste. For example: my childhood home was a brick house where even the smallest creak could be heard at night. The house often smelled of pine from the wooden furniture in the lounge room. The cool bricks gave the house a crisp feeling in the winter, but my mother's cooking always brought warmth.

Organising your story by place ultimately recognises that identity is formed not only by events, but by your environment. In many ways, our sense of self is shaped by the town we grew up in, the home we lived in, and the cultural influences that surrounded us. By structuring your book around those locations, you demonstrate how those places may have shaped the person you became.

Practical Example: Applying the Structure

Suggested chapter outline:

- Chapter 1: The home where I grew up
- Chapter 2: The town that shaped my childhood
- Chapter 3: Leaving home for the first time
- Chapter 4: The place where I built my career
- Chapter 5: The home where I raised my family
- Chapter 6: The place I now call home

Suggested opening sentence:

"Some places stay with you long after you have left them, and the town where I grew up is one of those places."

Suggested chapter structure:

- Begin by describing the location itself, including what it looked like and what daily life felt like there.
- Introduce the people who shared that place with you, such as family members, friends, or neighbours.
- Share memories or experiences that occurred in that setting.
- Reflect on how that place influenced your values, outlook, or direction in life.
- Conclude by explaining why that location remains meaningful when looking back.

Relationship based structure

A relationship-based structure organises your legacy book around the people who have shaped your life. In this approach, each chapter centres on a significant relationship such as parents, siblings, a partner, children, mentors, friends, colleagues, and even those with whom the relationship was complex or difficult.

This structure can feel particularly natural in legacy writing because, for many readers, relationships are what matter most. A chapter devoted to your mother, for example, may explore not only who she was but how her values influenced your own. A chapter on your partner may trace the evolution of your relationship, the challenges you navigated together, and the ways in which you both changed over time. Practically, within each chapter, you can still move chronologically or thematically as needed, but the central thread remains based on the relationship.

A relationship-based structure also creates emotional depth for the reader. It may express gratitude, clarify misunderstandings, acknowledge growth, or articulate love in a way that may not have been fully known at the time. For future generations they come to understand not just the events of your life, but the connections that defined it that may still exist within their own lives.

Practical Example: Applying the Structure

Suggested chapter outline:

- Chapter 1: My parents and the home they created
- Chapter 2: Siblings and growing up together
- Chapter 3: Friends who shaped my younger years
- Chapter 4: The person who became my partner
- Chapter 5: Becoming a parent
- Chapter 6: Relationships that influenced my path

Suggested opening sentence:

"Some of the earliest influences in my life came from my parents, whose guidance shaped the way I began to understand the world."

Suggested chapter structure:

- Begin by introducing the person or people and how they entered your life.
- Describe what the relationship was like during that period of your life.
- Share memories, interactions or moments that capture the nature of the relationship.
- Reflect on how the relationship influenced your decisions, thinking or values.
- Conclude by considering what that relationship means to you now.

Question/ answer structure

A question-and-answer structure organises your legacy book around meaningful questions. These may be questions that you have decided yourself or others asked by your children, grandchildren, or family members.

This structure may contain questions such as *What shaped your values? What was your most difficult time in your life? What are you most proud of? What would you do differently? What do you hope we remember about you?* When a reader sees a question on the page, it can feel as though they are participating in the dialogue. The answers to the questions are then written in a reflective format. For readers, this format often feels personal and the conversation can reflect on the kinds of discussions families wish they had more often.

Practically, this approach can be as simple or as layered as you choose. Each question may lead to a short reflection, or to a longer account that includes stories, context, and hindsight. Some questions may overlap, revealing recurring themes in your life. This structure can often surface insights more than a chronological story would overlook because the writing is tailored to each specific question.

A legacy book organised around questions acknowledges that understanding a life is not about reading it from start to finish, but about asking what mattered and taking the time to answer those questions thoughtfully.

Practical Example: Applying the Structure

Suggested chapter outline:

- Chapter 1: Where did our family story begin?
- Chapter 2: What was my childhood like?

- Chapter 3: What challenges shaped my life?
- Chapter 4: How did I meet my partner?
- Chapter 5: What lessons did life teach me?
- Chapter 6: What would I want future generations to understand?

Suggested opening sentence:

"One question I am often asked is what my childhood was like, and the answer begins in a small home where much of my early life unfolded."

Suggested chapter structure:

- Begin by acknowledging the question and why it is meaningful to address.
- Provide context or background that helps the reader understand the situation.
- Share memories or experiences that form the main part of the answer.
- Reflect on what you learned or how the experience influenced you.
- Conclude by summarising the perspective you now hold.

General traits structure

A general traits structure organises your legacy book around your defining qualities. These will be those traits and qualities that are distinctively recognisable as belonging to us from our loved ones.

In structuring your book, each chapter may focus on a trait which then explores how that manifested across different stages of life. These might include traits such as curiosity, resilience, independence, or creativity. For example, a chapter on resilience might include childhood experiences of overcoming setbacks, professional challenges later in life, or a health challenge. In this way, a single chapter may shift between different decades or contexts, because the trait is the theme rather than the timeline. A final chapter may be included regarding general likes and dislikes such as favourite movies, music, literature or foods.

By writing your book this way, your individual characteristics and voice explain the kind of person you are. This structure is particularly well suited to writers who are comfortable reflecting on their own personality and motivations. By the end of the book readers should be able to piece together your personality and how that reacted to the events within your life.

Practical Example: Applying the Structure

Suggested chapter outline:

- Chapter 1: Curiosity – the desire to understand the world
- Chapter 2: Determination – continuing when things were difficult
- Chapter 3: Humour – finding lightness in everyday life
- Chapter 4: Loyalty – the importance of standing by others
- Chapter 5: Resilience – recovering from life's challenges
- Chapter 6: Gratitude – appreciating what life has offered

- Chapter 7: General Traits – The things that I liked/ disliked

Suggested opening sentence:

"Throughout my life, one quality that has quietly guided many of my decisions is determination."

Suggested chapter structure:

- Begin by introducing the trait and why it has been meaningful in your life.
- Share experiences from different stages of life where this quality became visible.
- Reflect on how the trait influenced your decisions or responses to situations.
- Consider how this quality developed or strengthened over time.
- Conclude by explaining how you now understand this part of your character.

Objects based structure

An object-based structure organises your legacy book around meaningful items. In this approach, each chapter begins with a physical object - something you can hold and see. It may be a photograph, a wedding ring, a watch, a handwritten letter, a recipe book, a uniform, a diary, or even something seemingly ordinary that carries significance.

This structure can be especially powerful because objects often hold a history of being associated with more than one story or person. For example, a family heirloom such as a wedding ring may carry stories that predate your own life or generations.

This structure offers a gentle entry point for writers who are uncertain where to begin. The format can be flexible as each item brings forward the time associated with its memory. Alternatively, you may use a chronological structure but then refer to objects in order.

An object-based structure recognises that legacy is often preserved physically before it is preserved in writing. By choosing the items that have mattered to you the most, future readers are invited to connect with you in a unique way.

Practical Example: Applying the Structure

Suggested chapter outline:

- Chapter 1: The photograph from my childhood
- Chapter 2: The watch my father gave me
- Chapter 3: A letter that changed my direction
- Chapter 4: The house key from my first home
- Chapter 5: A small object that travelled through the years
- Chapter 6: The objects I hope will remain

Suggested opening sentence:

"Some objects appear ordinary at first glance, yet they quietly hold the stories of entire chapters of life. The first is a photograph from my childhood. I remember the exact day it was taken."

Suggested chapter structure:

- Begin by describing the object and where it came from.
- Explain why it was meaningful at the time you received or encountered it.
- Share the memories or experiences associated with it.
- Reflect on what the object represents now.
- Conclude by acknowledging why this item remains significant in your life story.

Before/ after structure

A before and after structure organises your legacy book around a single event or experience that tells a story of what came before and what came after. The event itself can be anything, such as a marriage, a separation, a diagnosis, entering public life, becoming a parent, or choosing a path that permanently redirected your future. It doesn't focus on the scale of the event but the change it produced.

This structure creates a natural contrast within your book. Readers may observe who you were before an event such as through your initial ambitions or assumptions, and then trace how you evolved over time. Where photographs are available, they can strengthen the contrast, for example a childhood photo placed alongside one taken in adulthood, or a wedding photograph set next to later family images can be a fascinating reflection of the impact of time.

For the writer, this structure encourages a particular kind of honesty. It asks you to sit with two versions of yourself and to reflect on what changed between them. Some writers find this the most clarifying structure of all, because it condenses their life to view how much they have grown both physically and mentally.

Ultimately, a before and after structure recognises that most lives are defined by the moments that divided time into then and now. By organising your story around those moments, you give future readers an honest account of how it changed you.

Practical Example: Applying the Structure

Suggested chapter outline:

- Chapter 1: Life before the turning point
- Chapter 2: The moment everything changed
- Chapter 3: The immediate aftermath

- Chapter 4: Adjusting to a new reality
- Chapter 5: The long-term changes that followed
- Chapter 6: What I understand about that moment now

Suggested opening sentence:

"Looking back now, there was a time when life felt steady and predictable, before events unfolded in ways I could not have anticipated."

Suggested chapter structure:

- Begin by describing what life was like before the event occurred.
- Introduce the moment or experience that created the turning point.
- Reflect on how you responded at the time and what you were thinking or feeling.
- Describe how life gradually changed in the period that followed.
- Conclude by explaining how you now understand that moment.

Hybrid structure (combining structures)

A hybrid structure recognises that a story may not fit neatly into any single approach. Rather than committing to one framework, it draws on a combination of structures by using whichever feels most natural at each part of your story. You might open with a chronological account of your early years, include a letter to your children, and then return to the timeline. The structure follows the story rather than the other way around.

This approach is more common than it might seem. Many of the most readable memoirs and legacy books do not strictly follow a single model. For writers who have spent time considering the structures outlined in this section, a hybrid approach often emerges naturally when none of the options meet what vision you have for what you want to say. The reader will not notice the shift in structure; they will simply notice that it fits you.

PART 4 – START WRITING

TIME TO START WRITING

There comes a point in every legacy project when the preparation must give way to action. You have reflected on why you want to write, considered who you are writing for, thought through emotional readiness, and taken into account some practical and legal considerations. But at some stage, the only way a book gets written is by actually attempting to write it.

Many people delay beginning a book because they believe that the opening needs to be perfect. When writing a legacy book, you are not attempting to produce a literary masterpiece - you are documenting a life, and that process can be imperfect. It is okay if your book has a typo here or there, if chapters don't follow a logical sequence and if some sections feel less polished than others. The purpose is not about perfection but about the preservation of your voice and the story you leave behind in your own words.

This section of the book is designed to remove the unnecessary pressure from writing. In the last section we examined the various ways you can structure your book and as you saw, you do not need to start in chronological order, you can move forward in a way that feels manageable to you. There may be moments when writing feels natural because those stories have been told many times before. There will be other times when it may feel extremely difficult because you need more time to sit with any feelings before they are ready to be written down.

Writing is not easy, but the hardest part is starting. Continuing to write is more about commitment. You do not need to write every single day and once you have formed the habit your book accumulates gradually. Overall, your book may be initially written imperfectly, but it is then revised and shaped over time until it reflects your voice telling the story.

Below is some practical guidance on how to choose a starting point, develop momentum without overwhelm, and keep going even when the process feels uncertain.

The first page problem

For many people, the most difficult page of a legacy book is the first. Most writers fear that whatever is written first must set the tone for everything that follows. In commercial publishing, that may be true but in legacy writing, it is not. Your first page does not need to be profound, it does not need to impress anyone, it only needs to begin the story.

When starting the first page it is natural to assume that it must start with a chronological structure as if that is the rule rather than an option. But the first page can start under any structure. It can begin with a moment of change, a decision, or a loss. It can even begin with a simple statement such as, "I am writing this because…" and allow the rest to unfold from there.

Perfectionism often disguises itself as preparation. You may find yourself reorganising notes, refining chapter headings, or rereading earlier sections of this guide instead of writing. These actions feel productive, but they are often ways of postponing starting due to feeling vulnerable about writing something you will share with others. Writing about your own life requires a degree of exposure, even if the audience is limited to family. The first page represents the moment you move from thinking about your story to making it exist and that shift can feel significant.

One way to overcome the first page problem is to remove its importance entirely. Give yourself permission to write a 'temporary beginning' Label it clearly if you need to. Tell yourself that this page may never remain as the opening of the book. In fact, many writers return to rewrite their first page only after the final chapter has been completed. Once the full shape of the story is visible, the introduction can become clearer.

Another approach is to lower your expectations. Instead of trying to craft an opening chapter, write a single memory by either describing one room, one conversation or one decision. Write without worrying about perfecting the structure. It may also help to remember that your legacy book is documenting experience. If your opening is straightforward, that is enough. In time, you may look back at your first page and see its imperfections but it does not need to be final.

The first page problem is solved by action. Once you start, the second page becomes easier, then so does the third. Begin imperfectly, and begin knowing that you can return to fix it later. The only page that cannot be improved is the one that was never written.

Choose a structure as your starting point

One of the most common assumptions about writing a legacy book is that it must begin at the beginning at birth, then to childhood, schooling, and to the first job. The familiar chronology feels orderly and safe. For some writers, this structure works beautifully and it provides a natural progression for memories to unfold in sequence. But it is important to understand that chronology is a choice.

Choosing your starting point is about momentum where you can begin and have the confidence to keep going. The best place to find that momentum is in whichever memory feels the most vivid and whatever structure fits that memory the best.

As detailed in the previous section, there are a range of structures available to you. A decade structure feels more natural as you move through your years as grouped periods. Within each decade you can draw from different stages of life, such as family, work, faith, friendships, setbacks, achievements, values. This approach can explore depth without feeling the pressure of exact dates.

Other writers may choose to begin with a thematic event such as a decision that altered their direction. In that structure chapters take shape from a specific moment and what that taught them in life. Alternatively, you may begin with a letter. Writing directly to the person or people you are creating this book for can soften the formality of the task. A simple opening such as, "If you are reading this, I want you to understand…" creates connection before the book can widen into chapters and themes.

There is also the option of beginning with the present. Writing about where you stand now with what you have learned, what you believe and what you understand differently than you once did. The present often offers perspective that earlier years did not so starting here can make earlier chapters easier to frame.

It is also worth acknowledging that some periods may feel emotionally heavier than others. You do not to start with the most difficult chapter. In fact, it is often wiser not to. Beginning with the sections that feel steady builds the confidence and the habit of writing that will carry you toward the chapters that require more from you.

If you are unable to choose a structure, consider making a list of moments that feel significant. These may be decisions, conversations, events, regrets, proud achievements or unexpected outcomes. Notice which one carries the most energy when you are writing it down. That is likely to be your starting point.

The right place to begin is wherever you feel that you can write continually and build on. Remember that chapters can be rearranged later. What matters now is that you choose a place for you to move forward rather than hesitate. Once you start, the rest of the story can follow.

Create a simple chapter structure before you write

Before you begin drafting full chapters, it is helpful to create a simple framework that will guide your writing without constraining it. A basic chapter outline acts as a container that gives your memories somewhere to sit. Placing chapter titles acts like a working map to guide your writing.

Once you have chosen your structure begin by writing the headings of each potential chapter on a separate page of your word document. You then start writing one segment at a time. At this stage, resist the urge to make the structure perfect. What you are creating is a working outline, not a published contents page. Chapters can later be rearranged, merged, or removed as the draft develops. Many writers discover that the structure only becomes clear after several chapters have been drafted. The outline is there to get you started not to lock you into decisions.

Depending on the structure you have chosen, it may also help to include one guiding question beneath each proposed chapter heading, for example: What did I believe at this time? What was I afraid of? What changed because of this? What did I not understand then that I understand now? These prompts will keep your writing on track and prevent chapters from reducing the information to simple summaries of events.

A chapter structure serves another important purpose. When you can see the shape of the book, even roughly, it becomes less daunting as you are no longer facing an undefined task, you are instead working through identifiable sections. Remember that the goal is momentum, a modest framework will support your writing far more effectively than attempting to start on a blank page. Once it exists, you are no longer asking, "Where do I begin?" You are asking, "Which section will I work on today?"

Write as you speak

One of the most common shifts that occurs when people begin writing their life story is a subtle change in voice. The language becomes more formal, sentences become longer and more complicated, and words are chosen because they sound impressive. This instinct is understandable. Writing can feel official, permanent, and therefore serious. However, a legacy book is different as it is meant to be written in your voice which carries with it a particular rhythm of how you think and speak.

Writing as you speak refers to allowing your natural rhythm, vocabulary, and tone to remain intact when writing your book. The way you would retell a story, explain a decision, or reflect quietly on a memory often carries warmth and authenticity that can be lost when you try to write it to 'sound like an author.' Your readers are not looking for literary performance -they are looking to be able to hold onto you.

If you find yourself using phrases you would never say aloud, pause and read the paragraph back to yourself. Does it sound like you? Would your children, your partner, or your closest friends recognise your voice in those words? If not, simplify it. Replace formal language with the words you would normally use. For example, instead of writing, "At that juncture in my professional trajectory, I encountered significant adversity," you might write, "At that point in my career, things became difficult." The second version may feel less elaborate, but it is far easier to read and trust.

Your natural speaking style is part of your legacy and it is something that cannot be manufactured. If writing feels difficult, consider speaking your memories aloud and recording them. You may discover that your voice flows more easily when you are not staring at a blank screen or typing. You can later transcribe and edit the spoken words, refining them without stripping away their authenticity. The simplest test is this: if someone who knows you well read a page without seeing your name, would they recognise it as yours? If the answer is yes, you are on the right path.

Momentum vs perfection

At this stage of writing, there may be friction between attempting to write more through momentum and refining what is already written by attempting to make sure it is perfect. Most legacy books stall here because the desire to refine overtakes the need to continue. The desire to improve on what has already been written can feel more like progress, but it often slows or stops the work that has been done completely.

Perfectionism presents itself as high standards by insisting every paragraph is polished before moving onto the next one. It works on the idea that the book must first exist as complete before it can be shaped properly. On the other hand, momentum is what keeps the work moving toward completion. A chapter drafted imperfectly still advances the work, but the goal is not literary precision, it is the forward movement to complete the book even if it isn't perfect. The problem arises when you pause repeatedly to edit what you have just written, you disrupt the movement of completing it. Each time you return to earlier pages it often brings a different viewpoint and the cycle continues.

To overcome this, it is helpful to consciously separate drafting from refining. Drafting is the process of writing your book in full first. It may be full of imperfection, repetition, and incomplete phrasing. Once it is written you then focus on refining it by selecting when you clarify, rewrite or remove. These are different tasks, and they are most effective when they are not performed simultaneously. Give yourself permission to write your draft freely, knowing that the perfection will come later at the editing stage. Allow imperfection to exist temporarily. Your book is completed by moving forward one page at a time, and in time, those pages eventually form into something complete.

Writer's block

At some point in the writing process, momentum will slow down, words may feel harder to surface, you may sit down with the intention to write and find yourself reorganising notes instead, or the initial clarity that made you begin will change to questioning its worth. This is often described as writer's block.

Writer's block is frequently misunderstood as the absence of ideas, but it can be for a number of reasons. When you are writing about your own life, you are not only constructing sentences; you are revisiting experiences, reassessing decisions, and sometimes confronting unresolved emotion. That work can require energy and periods of slower writing can often indicate that reflections are still occurring beneath the surface.

Alternatively, it might be associated with the pressure to be accurate, fair, articulate and to complete the book quickly. When these expectations arise, your mind becomes cautious rather than expressive, hesitant rather than active. If you encounter a block, it can help to reduce the scale of the task rather than stopping entirely. Instead of drafting a full chapter, write a single memory or instead of composing paragraphs, answer a guiding question. These small shifts can restore movement. It may also help to change to a different chapter temporarily.

There may be deeper moments of blockage, particularly when approaching chapters that involve conflict, regret, or loss. In these instances, writer's block can be a protective response. If that occurs, consider writing privately about the emotion without intending to include it in the final book. It is also important to recognise that some blocks are physical rather than emotional. Fatigue, competing responsibilities, illness, or family commitments may interrupt rhythm.

A legacy book does not demand urgency. A pause of weeks or even months does not erase what you have written. This is not a race against a deadline-it is a long-form act of preservation. Understand that blocks are part of the rhythm of meaningful work. The writing resumes not because you forced it, but because you allowed space for it.

Writing as a record vs writing to process

Not all writing serves the same purpose. In a legacy book, there is an important distinction between writing to record and writing to process something. Writing the record preserves the external shape of your life and writing to process deepens its meaning. Understanding the difference between the two can shape both how you approach the work and how you decide what ultimately belongs in the final book.

Writing to record draws on factual memory, it answers questions such as: What happened? When did it occur? Who was involved? What decisions were made? This type of writing creates an account of the events which preserves facts, timelines, and milestones for future readers who may otherwise have relied on second-hand stories.

Writing to process is reflective in nature. It is the part of the legacy book that explores questions such as: How did I feel at the time? What did I not understand then that I see now? Why did this affect me so deeply? This type of writing interprets experiences with the benefit of hindsight and maturity. It is often the case that this writing becomes less about informing others about what has happened and more about clarifying your own understanding.

When you begin drafting, you may find that process writing naturally precedes record writing. As you describe an event, emotions or unresolved questions may surface. You might write far more than you intend, circling around the same memory from multiple angles. It is often a sign that you are engaging with the material and processing can be part of the writing journey, even if not all of it remains in the final version.

If you notice yourself feeling overwhelmed while drafting, pause and ask yourself: am I recording, or am I processing? If you are processing, consider whether this is a draft for yourself rather than for the book. You can always return later to transform that reflection into a chapter that serves the reader. Ultimately, the two forms of writing work together to create your legacy book. One provides structure and the other provides insight. When balanced carefully, they create a legacy that is both informative and thoughtful.

Writing scenes vs summaries

As you begin drafting chapters, you will notice that some passages are summaries and move quickly to cover years in a few sentences, while others will slow down to a scene and linger on a single moment. For a legacy book, summaries and scenes should work together -summaries provide structure and momentum while scenes provide depth and emotional connection.

A summary condenses events. It is useful for background, transitions or to move the story forward efficiently. For example: "In 2003, we moved to Brisbane for work and the transition was harder than I expected." In one sentence, time advances and context is established.

By contrast, a scene slows the story and the reader enters into a specific moment. In relation to the above example, it might detail the conversation at the kitchen table about the move, the hesitation before accepting the job, the child asking whether they would see their friends again, the quiet drive to the new house. The purpose of a scene is to create emotional depth to allow the reader not just to understand what happened, but what it felt like to be there.

A legacy book may lean heavily on summary because it feels safer and more efficient. However, this can make the book feel distant, more like a timeline than a lived experience. Including even one scene can transform the writing. Overall, the aim is to capture the essence of the moment so that the reader can reflect on your life's journey and understand it through your eyes.

Case Example

Consider the same memory written two different ways:

As a summary

My father was a quiet man who showed love through actions rather than words. He worked long hours but always made time for us after work. I remember him teaching me things and feeling grateful for his patience.

As a scene

On Monday afternoons I would come downstairs after my favourite cartoon had finished. My father would have my homework ready to review and open across the kitchen table and have a mug of tea waiting for me beside his. We would then go through the questions together. Whenever id get stuck, he would give me a hint or two to try and help me but would never tell me the answers. He never lost patience no matter how many times I thought id have the answer, he would just nod and smile. I remember the smell of his coffee and the tired lines he had under his eyes. Those afternoons made me feel like I was able to do my homework correctly and I always felt confident when I turned it in. I remember he would always go into the study after and open his laptop and he would still be working by the time I went to bed. I was always grateful for his help and I would always show him my marks to let him know how much he helped me.

Writing dialogue carefully

Dialogue can enhance a legacy book. However, many writers hesitate to include dialogue because they worry about accuracy. It is important to understand very few people can recall conversations word for word, particularly those that occurred years or decades ago.

When you are writing a legacy book, you are not required to repeat conversations with verbatim accuracy. Instead, try to capture the substance and tone of what was said. If you remember the essence of a conversation but not the precise wording, you can signal this gently with phrases such as, "I remember him saying something like…," or "The conversation went roughly along these lines…" Both of these statements make it clear that you are reconstructing the moment without claiming precision.

Dialogue is particularly useful when writing about pivotal events such as moments of decision, conflict, or encouragement. A short exchange can reveal far more about a relationship than a summary. For example, rather than writing, "My father was reluctant about the decision," you might include a remembered line that conveys his hesitation such as "my father said to me that it would be the wrong decision to make but I didn't listen to him".

It is also wise to avoid recreating lengthy conversations unless they are central to the narrative. A legacy book benefits from being selective. A few carefully placed lines of dialogue will feel more natural for you than writing pages of reconstructed conversation. For the reader, the dialogue works best when it highlights something essential such as a decision, a misunderstanding, a moment of humour, or a change in direction.

Dialogue should be used with care, especially when recounting conflict. Avoid exaggerating or sharpening words to strengthen your own position. Time can distort memory, particularly when emotions are involved. If you are unsure whether your recollection may be clouded by feeling, pause and consider whether the line reflects the spirit of the exchange rather than the most dramatic interpretation of it.

Where sensitivity exists, particularly when describing conversations with living individuals, caution becomes important. You are writing from your perspective, and you are entitled to that perspective, but at the same time you are acknowledging that others may have experienced the exchange differently. To acknowledge this you might write, "From my perspective, it felt as though…" signals that you are writing from your own experience without claiming that your version is the only accurate one.

Writing the ordinary

One of the most common hesitations in legacy writing is the belief that only extraordinary events should be recorded. People assume that unless their lives were marked by public achievement, dramatic hardship, or historic moments, there is little worth preserving. Yet when families return to your book years later, it is rarely the headline events that they will cherish most, it is the ordinary details.

The ordinary is in the rhythm of mornings, the way the house felt in winter, the meals that were passed down by the generations and the routines that seemed insignificant at the time but, in hindsight, formed the structure of family life. These details may not have felt monumental when they occurred, but they are often the details that reveal your character clearly. That is not to say that you need to devote entire chapters to routine, but you may choose to weave ordinary details into larger story.

Examples of writing about the ordinary may include:

- When describing a career decision, include what a typical day at work involved.
- When writing about raising children, describe the atmosphere of the household.
- When reflecting on a particular decade, recall the music you listened to in the background.
- When describing your home town, include what your weekly routine was like.

In many ways, writing the ordinary acknowledges that legacy is also built through the repeated, often unseen acts. For those who come after you, those details may become the most cherished parts of all because they exist nowhere else.

<table>
<tr><td>

Case Example

Without attention to the ordinary:
We had a family routine that we followed most days. Meals were important to us and we usually ate together. Those times were the happy ones that I look back on fondly.

With attention to the ordinary:
Tea was at six o'clock and that was not negotiable. We would all squeeze around a table that was slightly too small for five people. The TV would stay on while we ate but nobody watched it. Conversation would move between what had happened during the day and our plans for the next day. When the talk turned to holidays, the table got louder. Everyone had an opinion and nobody waited their turn to share it.

</td></tr>
</table>

Knowing when a chapter is done

One of the quieter challenges in writing a legacy book is finishing a chapter. You may find yourself wondering whether it is long enough, whether the writing requires further explanation or whether another paragraph might improve the chapter further. At this stage, perfectionism tends to take over. While careful editing has its place, endless revisiting can prevent progress.

A chapter is 'done' when you feel that its message has been conveyed. To determine whether you have done that you may ask yourself: Have I explained what happened clearly? Have I described why it mattered? Have I acknowledged what I understood at the time and What I understand now? If the answers are yes, the chapter may be complete.

It is also helpful to recognise that depth does not always equal length. The periods of life that were steady and uncomplicated may only require a few pages, while periods that were more transformative will naturally demand more space. Having a short chapter is not a negative thing if the meaning has been carried with it.

When a chapter is reaching a natural conclusion, you find that the writing begins to circle, and you may find yourself making the same points in a different way. As the points have been made continuing to write will only add volume without building on the chapter's message. When this occurs, it is often a sign that the chapter has said what it needs to say.

Completing a chapter should also feel settled. Some chapters will remain bittersweet or unresolved by the very nature of the message. If you get to the end of a chapter and it doesn't feel complete have a few days' distance and return with fresh eyes. A little distance can confirm whether the chapter holds together or whether a small addition is needed.

Finally, trust that the reader does not require absolute completeness to understand your story. A chapter is done when it carries the message of your story and when you are able to move forward without the sense that something essential has been left unsaid. At that point, allow it to stand as finished.

Trusting the future reader

When writing a legacy book, it is natural to imagine how your words will be received. You may picture your children, grandchildren, partner, or even readers you have never met and wonder whether they will agree with your decisions, understand your reasoning, or judge you for what you have written. These thoughts can subconsciously shape the tone of your book and may result in softening the language, over-explaining choices, or removing certain reflections altogether.

Trusting the future reader is about adopting the mindset that those who will read your book will do so with curiosity rather than criticism. It is important to remember that a legacy book is not typically opened with hostility, it is opened because someone wants to understand you more and that desire alone creates a positive starting point.

When writing about difficult periods in your life, there may be sections where you are unsure how your account will be received. Writers often assume they must defend every decision and they will add layers of justification to ensure they are not misunderstood. Trusting the future reader asks you to trust most people understand that decisions you made may have been done with limited information, under pressure, or within the constraints of a particular era.

To manage these circumstances, it is important to be reasonably clear on how you felt. You may something like "At the time I believed this was the right path for me," or "Looking back, I see it differently now", this provides insight into softening difficult times. Acknowledge that others may have seen events differently and then allow the reader to hold that complexity without over-managing their response.

Trusting the reader also extends in the opposite direction as well. Future readers bring their own maturity, context, and life experience to the page. A child reading your book at twenty will understand it differently at forty or a grandchild reading decades later may see strength where you saw struggle. You do not need to anticipate every interpretation as the meaning will differ depending on the individual reader.

Writing indirectly asks for trust. When writing your legacy book, you offer your voice and the reader listens to that perspective. You cannot control their conclusions, but you can trust that the reader who opens the book will recognise you in it.

SEEKING ADDITIONAL SUPPORT

For some writers, Part 4 will carry them all the way to a completed draft. For others, only a partial draft may emerge because the task feels heavier than was originally anticipated. This is not a sign of failure but indicates that writing about your own life can be harder than writing about other things. Writing a legacy book can be deeply personal work. It asks you to recall memory, reflect on those memories, and find the patience to keep writing.

While some people prefer to work entirely independently, others may benefit from guidance or technical assistance. There are many forms of help available. Some writers may seek feedback from a trusted friend or family member. Some may prefer to be interviewed and have their story transcribed and then shape it professionally. Others may work with an editor to refine the language and structure once the draft is complete. Regardless of the method, seeking support does not make your book any less authentic, it simply makes it more likely to get finished.

It is important to release the idea that writing must be done alone to be accepted. Throughout history, memoirs and biographies have often involved editors, collaborators, and interviewers. What matters is that your voice remains central and that external support shapes your voice but it does not replace it. In the below section, we will explore the different ways you might access additional help, and how to choose the level of support that aligns with your goals and capacity. Whether you continue independently or invite others into the process, the aim remains the same: to bring your story to completion.

Dictation tools

Not everyone finds it easy to write by typing. Physical fatigue, injury, or time constraints can make extended periods at a keyboard difficult — and for some, thoughts simply flow more naturally when spoken aloud. Dictation tools can provide a practical and accessible alternative for you to speak your memories aloud and convert them into written text.

When you use dictation to talk through memories, you may find that it unlocks a different rhythm where details can surface more freely. For legacy writing in particular, this can be a strength. Most modern devices include built-in voice-to-text features that can transcribe speech directly into a document or note. Even recording on your phone can be enough to get started and the recording can later be transcribed manually or through transcription software.

It can be helpful to outline a basic structure before you start using dictation tools. Before you begin speaking, identify the chapter you intend to cover and consider jotting down a few bullet points to guide you. Alternatively, you may ask yourself questions and then answer them aloud. Without this direction, you may find that your thoughts begin to drift. A loose outline keeps the story focused while still giving you room to be spontaneous.

There are also some practical considerations to keep in mind when using dictation tools including:

- Choose a quiet environment to improve transcription accuracy
- Speak clearly and at a moderate pace
- You may find it helpful to imagine you are speaking directly to the person they are writing for
- Review the text soon after recording while the memory of what you intended to say is still fresh
- Make small corrections early to prevent confusion later.

When using dictation tools, accept that the first transcript will likely be imperfect. Speech patterns will differ from written language, however the purpose of using dictation is to capture enough substance to work from, with editing to come later.

If typing has started to feel like hard work, dictation is worth trying. It can take the pressure off and, may bring out a more natural voice. Remember that the story remains yours whether written by hand, typed at a desk, or spoken and transcribed - it is just another way of telling it.

Reach out to family members

Writing a legacy book is often thought of as a individual project, however, it can become a meaningful opportunity to involve the people who share parts of your story. Family members can help in many ways from offering practical assistance by helping you recall details, gather materials and give you encouragement throughout the writing journey.

One of the most valuable ways family can contribute is by helping to reconstruct memories. While your perspective remains central to the book, relatives may remember small details that bring the stories to life such as the setting of a family event, or the sequence in which things unfolded. Family members can also assist by locating materials that can support the story such as photographs, letters or certificates, that are often scattered across different households.

Reaching out to family can also deepen the sense that the book belongs not only to you but to the broader family story. When relatives understand that the purpose of the book is to preserve memories for future generations, they are often willing to contribute along the way. These conversations themselves can become meaningful moments of reflection and connection. A family's contributions may not shape every page, they often help strengthen the depth of the story being written.

Hiring support

There may come a point in writing your legacy book where starting or finishing feels harder than you anticipated. A solution may be hiring professional support depending on what you need. This may be an editor to structure and refine a completed draft or it might be hiring a writing coach who can guide you through the drafting process. I established Legacy Impact Australia because I understood from my own experience that many people want to tell their story but they are unsure about how to do it. Professional support exists to close that gap.

Before seeking support, consider what you need. Some writers may only require light editorial refinement while others will benefit from more comprehensive support to guide the project. In either case ensure you are clear about the assistance you require in order to choose the right level of support you need. The person assisting you should understand that their role is to amplify your voice and not replace it.

If hiring support, transparency about process, expectations, and costs is equally important. It is also acceptable to seek support in stages. You may draft independently and later engage an editor or you may record your reflections and then hire someone to transcribe and organise them. Support does not need to be all-encompassing to be effective.

Ultimately, the decision to hire assistance reflects a commitment to completing your legacy. It acknowledges that preserving a life story is significant enough to want extra care. Whether you complete the manuscript alone or with guidance, the purpose remains unchanged - to create a considered and lasting account of your life.

CLOSING

If you are reading this final chapter, you have taken steps to think about taking your legacy seriously. This book has taken you through the desire of wanting to write a book to doing it. You have considered how to start, how to structure your chapters, how to maintain momentum, and how to seek support if needed. At this point, the task is no longer just a concept, it is a practical action you can take.

If there is one truth that underpins this entire book, it is this: your legacy book does not need to be perfect. At some point, you will close your own manuscript. You may still see imperfections. You may still think of details you could have added. No written account captures a life in full but what you will have created is a considered record, a bridge between generations, a steady explanation of who you were and how you understood your world.

A legacy book remains for present and future generations. Someone will open the pages because of curiosity and love. They will look for understanding, they will search for context and they will want to hear from you. This book has guided you through the process - the legacy itself is yours to leave.

ABOUT THE AUTHOR

I am an Australian writer with a background in government, policy, and legal publishing. For most of my professional life I have worked with complex information — analysing it, shaping it into written form, and communicating it clearly to people who needed to understand it. That work taught me a great deal about the difference between information that is technically present and information that actually reaches the person it was meant for.

I developed a strong interest in preserving personal stories and family histories after losing close family members and realising just how much an individual life impacts on others. I believe that the experiences of ordinary people, the challenges they faced, the values they lived by and the lessons they learned, hold enduring meaning for future generations.

This belief led me to creating *Legacy Impact Australia.* This work focuses on helping individuals capture their memories and reflections in a structured and thoughtful way, transforming lived experience into a lasting written legacy. There are two streams: personal and family legacies that preserve multi-generational stories and memories, and professional legacies that document careers, contributions, and institutional knowledge for senior professionals and organisations.

I live in Queensland with my family. The reason I do this work is simple. I want to ensure that the experiences and lessons of one generation can continue to guide and inspire the next.

LEGACY BOOK CHECKLIST

Step 1 – Why do you want to write your legacy book?
Tick all that apply:

☐ To be remembered

☐ To preserve family history

☐ To pass on lessons or inspire others

☐ To leave something personal

☐ To make meaning of your own life

☐ To correct the record

☐ To strengthen the connection with immediate family members

☐ Time feels limited

☐ Other ________________

Step 2 – Who are you writing your legacy book for?
Tick all that apply:

☐ Children

☐ Grandchildren or people not born yet

☐ Partner or close loved one

☐ Parents or elders

☐ For myself

☐ Other ________________

Step 3 – What do I want to write your legacy book about?
Tick all that apply:

☐ Recording a life story

☐ Recording a focused story or particular life event

☐ Recording your professional life

☐ Record life lessons and wisdom

☐ Record an integrated legacy of professional and personal life experiences

☐ Record General Traits

☐ Record for the future and not the past

☐ Record expressions of love

☐ Recording a tangible history

☐ Other ___________________

Step 4 – Practical considerations:

Does my story raise any matters of – Tick all that apply

☐ Defamation

☐ Copyright

☐ Privacy

I will be – Tick all that apply:

☐ Changing names and details

☐ Using a disclaimer at the start of the book

☐ Including photos

☐ Other ___________________

Step 5 – Methods to collate my legacy book:

I have used the following methods to collate my legacy book – Tick all that apply:

☐ Memory mapping

☐ Memory boxes

☐ Photos

☐ Journaling

☐ Social media

☐ Other ___________________

Step 6 – Structure of my legacy book:

Tick all that apply:

☐ Chronological structure

☐ Decade structure

☐ Thematic (event) structure

☐ From the present-day structure

☐ Summary of lessons structure

☐ Letters within the structure

☐ Generational structure

☐ Place based structure

☐ Relationship based structure

☐ Question/ answer structure

☐ General traits structure

☐ Objects based structure

☐ Before/ after structure

☐ Hybrid structure

☐ Other ___________________